CRUDEN, Robert
THE NEGRO IN RECONSTRUCTION

Recent scholarship "has drastically altered our understanding of Reconstruction and of the black man's role in it," states Robert Cruden. As the book shows, the Negro's significant contributions as soldier and civilian in saving the Union and winning his freedom failed to alleviate the hostility of both North and South toward his new status as freedman. Struggling to shake off the bonds of a second-class citizenship, realistic black leaders were prepared to deal with the problems of power. But, as the author notes, they "wanted power to ends not yet socially accepted: schools for blacks, civil rights, suppression of racist violence." The painful process of opportunity and acceptance met black accomplishments in politics, education, religion, and labor in spite of an almost "universal white hostility." And even race relations improved as a result of legislation and change of attitude by the white majority. *The Author:* Robert Cruden is Professor of History at Lewis and Clark College. He is the author also of *James Ford Rhodes: The Man, The Historian and His Work.*

April, 1969, 192 pages, LC # 69-17370
A Spectrum Book

Cloth $5.95

D0445058

The Negro
in Reconstruction

ROBERT CRUDEN

A SPECTRUM BOOK

Prentice-Hall, Inc., *Englewood Cliffs, New Jersey*

Current printing (last number):
10 9 8 7 6 5 4 3 2 1

P 13–610873–3
C 13–610881–4

Library of Congress Catalog Card Number: 69–17370

Printed in the United States of America

Prentice-Hall International, Inc. (*London*)

For the Family:
Jan and Chris
Diana and Bob

Preface

Scholars in Reconstruction history will find here little that is new. This work is not for them, but for interested laymen and students. Its aim is to provide, in compact and readable form, an interpretation, based on recent scholarship, of a crucial period in our history. Such scholarship has drastically altered our understanding of Reconstruction and of the black man's role in it. Unfortunately, it appears that to the general reading public it is less well-known than the obsolete interpretations of James Ford Rhodes, William A. Dunning, and Claude Bowers.

This is not a comprehensive history of Reconstruction—not even of the Negro in Reconstruction. It does present, within the limits imposed by a short work, a view of many aspects of black-white relationships stemming from emancipation and of the problems that arose when it became clear to black men and to many white abolitionists that freedom in itself was not enough—that it must be accompanied by equality.

This has entailed some discussion of the general framework of the Reconstruction policy, but attention is focused on the black American and his attempts to find meaning in freedom. In one sense, that is what Reconstruction was all about—the role of the free black man in American society. That problem is still with us, in historically different circumstances. Even a brief glance at how men a century ago grappled with the issue may help illuminate the present.

I wish to express my appreciation of the help given me while I have been engaged in this work. Carl F. Wittke and the late Harvey Wish, both of Western Reserve University, encouraged my interest in the role of black Americans in Reconstruction. Two laymen, Louis Koren, M.D., of Birmingham, Michigan, and Jack Auringer of Detroit, Michigan, demonstrated that citizens, confronted with problems of our own day, are interested in the country's first experiment in integration. The anonymous reader for Prentice-Hall, Inc., contributed significantly through his helpful criticism of the original manuscript. I owe a special debt of gratitude to Martin D. Lewis of Sir George Williams University, Montreal, for providing the stimulus to write this book. My wife, Janet, showed more than her usual understanding during the troublesome period of literary gestation. Finally, my thanks to Mrs. Joanne Brumley of Lewis and Clark College for her aid in typing, and to President John R. Howard and the Trustees of the College for providing conditions which make it possible for a faculty member to research and write without injuring the interests of students.

ROBERT CRUDEN

Portland, Oregon
January, 1969

Contents

CHAPTER **1**

Why Congressional Reconstruction?

On April 15, 1865, a war-weary and far from unified American people, under the leadership of an "accidental President," had to assume the burden of meeting new problems—problems unprecedented in their nature and magnitude: restoration of the Union after a bitter and protracted war; adjustment to the forces of industrialism, the hegemony of which the war had assured; and, most important and difficult of all, accommodation to the role of the Negro as free man in American society. The attempts to solve all three converged and were fused in the process we call Reconstruction.

It was not a simple problem-solving situation. The problems in themselves were but dimly and partially perceived, and their attempted solutions were accompanied by desperate efforts to frustrate them. The whole process was in the hands of fallible human beings—politicians, businessmen, humanitarians, Southerners, Northerners, whites, blacks—driven by all kinds of motives, passions, and prejudices. As they sought their diverse ends, they fought and they compromised; yesterday's ally became today's enemy; lofty principle became entangled in political thickets; greed for money and greed for power reluctantly found themselves allied with abolitionists in a campaign to bring a new measure of dignity to men and women just out of slavery. In this lay the story of Reconstruction, dramatic, confused, intensely meaningful, as it moved through three distinct phases: Presidential Reconstruction (or "restoration") during 1865 and early 1866; the attempt at "moderate" Congressional Reconstruction in 1866; and finally, beginning in March, 1867, full Congressional Reconstruction. To understand this last phase, which is usually what is

1

meant by the term "Reconstruction," we must trace why the earlier phases failed.

Before undertaking that, however, let us note that in 1865 the great mass of Northerners was not much exercised over these problems; the ordinary citizen left such matters for his elected leaders to solve while he pursued more mundane affairs.

The worker was concerned with employment and living standards. During the war real wages fell by a third; now, competition for jobs, sharpened by rapid demobilization of the army and by renewed immigration, was made even worse by a post-war depression which lasted for 18 months. Insofar as Reconstruction touched the worker directly it was in the fear of an influx of skilled and unskilled Negro labor into Northern cities. For this, such skilled workers as were organized had an answer: exclusion of the Negro and imposition of the closed (white) shop on employers.

The farmer, caught in the collapse of his wartime market, was trapped also by the deflationary cycle which cut commodity prices 25 per cent by 1868 and by the need for extensive capital investment in new farm equipment without which farming, especially in the West, was economically impossible. His attention was given to paper money and to government regulation of railroads and grain elevators, agencies which cut his market by charging all the traffic would bear before his wheat, barley, and oats reached the urban and foreign consumer.

Members of the business community, engulfed like everyone else in the downward spiral, looked beyond to the prospects of railroad building, exploitation of western lands, tapping the untouched resources of the South, and renewed expansion of the manufacturing boom which had come with the war. Their primary political interests centered on the tariff, currency and credit, federal subsidies for railroad construction, a plentiful supply of labor, and free access to the nation's natural resources. However much they differed among themselves on these issues, they were united in wanting a speedy adjustment to peace. Reconstruction to them meant restoration of the national market and unrestricted opportunity to make good use of Southern coal, timber lands, and iron as well as to invest profitably in cotton plantations and railroads.

Only a handful of Northerners, typified by Senator Charles Sumner of Massachusetts, Representative Thaddeus Stevens of Pennsylvania, and Frederick Douglass, the former slave become abolitionist leader, were concerned with the fate of the Negro. Convinced that the white South would not accept the freedman as a *free man*, they looked upon Reconstruction as a process of training the Negro in the exercise of freedom under federal tutelage—on a civil, not a military, basis. Sumner and Douglass emphasized the need for black suffrage; Stevens sought to assure widespread Negro land ownership through federal auspices. In this way, he thought, the long term economic and political independence of the Negro would be protected.

White Southerners were more directly concerned with the problems of post-war policy than their Northern counterparts. Many of their farms, plantations, and towns were ravaged; markets for cotton were now contracted with the appearance of competitors from India and the Middle East; wealth in terms of billions of dollars had been wiped out through emancipation and the collapse of Confederate currency and securities. The future of every Southerner—farmer, planter, mechanic, businessman—was in the hands of the conqueror. Until the conqueror's will was known, the ordinary citizen devoted himself perforce to the problems of livelihood—and to the unavoidable problem of adjusting to the unaccustomed presence of black men, not as slaves, but as free men.

Yet it would be a mistake to assume that, because the masses of the citizenry returned gladly to the ways of peace, the memories and passions of the war had been subdued. Not so. The knife of war had cut too deeply to permit easy forgetfulness. The war was (and still is) the bloodiest in our history: more than 622,500 soldiers and sailors died in Union and Confederate service, compared to 405,000 American dead in World War II. When it is remembered that the population of 1860 was less than a fourth that of 1940, it is easy to understand the emotional impact of the war: hardly a household in the nation was left untouched, directly or indirectly. Each side bore the burden of a great grief; each blamed the other. Each side provided receptive audiences to the widespread tales of wartime atrocities and of the horrors of prisoner of war camps, Andersonville and Camp Douglas. In the North was added the deep revulsion over the assassination of Lincoln, who was never an object of reverence in his lifetime, but was already in process of transfiguration into a Christ-like victim of Confederate conspiracy.

Underneath the outward calm of a nation at peace once again ran deep feelings, quick to find public expression when aroused. Thus, Andrew Johnson, the new President, struck a responsive chord in the North and West when he reiterated his wartime view: "Treason must be made odious, and the traitor must be punished and impoverished." An Alabama planter voiced the sentiments of many white Southerners when he proclaimed: "I'm a foreigner. I scorn to be called a citizen of the United States. I shall take no oath [of allegiance], so help me God!" Few whites, in either North or South, genuinely shared the outlook of Petersburg,

Virginia, Negroes who resolved: "That we have no feeling of resentment toward our former owners, but we are willing to let the past be buried with the past, and in the future treat all persons with kindness and respect who shall treat us likewise."

It was Andrew Jackson Johnson's historic misfortune that the mantle of power fell on him at this critical juncture. An implacable foe of the Southern Establishment, he had made his way from illiterate poverty through the rough-and-tumble of Tennessee Democratic politics to national public office as the champion of the common man. During the war, as United States Senator and as military governor of Tennessee, he had so resolutely demonstrated devotion to the Union that he was named vice-president on the Lincoln Union Party ticket in 1864. Now 57 years old, he was grim, inflexible, quick to see in major political issues abstract principles which admitted of no compromise. As a historian sympathetic to him noted, "He did not know how to compromise. . . . He could bear insult, personal danger, obloquy; but he could not yield his point."

Indeed, his political success had been in large measure due to the fact that, as Eric McKitrick has pointed out, he was an "outsider" who was free to attack the Establishment because he had no personal or political ties with its members.[1] At the same time he possessed a loyal following among a host of other "outsiders"—farmers, shopkeepers, mechanics, mountaineers—whose aspirations, frustrations, and prejudices he embodied. Thus, by temperament and experience he was unfitted to guide the nation during a crisis when political skills of the highest order were called for.

To this was allied an outmoded Jacksonian social and political outlook which blinded him to the realities of American life in the 1860's. A true believer in the moral superiority of rural over urban life, he idealized the common man, particularly the yeoman farmer, as the repository of civic and domestic virtue. If the common man had not yet brought forth that democratic order in which Johnson passionately believed, it was because he was misled in the South by the planting aristocracy, in the North by business, and in both by politicians. Now that the planters had been overthrown, Johnson was confident the small farmers and mechanics in the South would take over the seats of the mighty.

But an even greater danger presented itself: an aristocracy of the dollar, based on New England finance and industry, threatened democracy

---

[1] Eric L. McKitrick, *Andrew Johnson and Reconstruction* (Chicago: University of Chicago Press, 1960), p. 85.

on a national scale. Against this threat of the "money power," Johnson would raise up the states as the only power capable of meeting the centralization of power in the national government sought by business. This doctrine goes far to explain Johnson's reliance on the states in his Reconstruction policy.

Regardless of the validity of Johnson's views, they were, in terms of practical politics, unwelcome to a nation plunging headlong into industrial and territorial expansion, technological development, urbanization, and political centralization. Johnson's attempts to practice what Kenneth Stampp calls the "politics of nostalgia" [2] inevitably brought him into conflict with the spokesmen for the new forces at work in American society.

His Jacksonian philosophy had perhaps an even greater flaw in view of the problems he confronted: it had some place for the Negro as a free man, but it had none for him as an equal. Johnson's quarrel with the Southern Establishment was based on antagonism to the plantation system, not on hostility to slavery as such. Indeed, in a curious demonstration of his "democratic" faith he had expressed the wish that every white family might have a slave for "drudgery and menial service." Later, he supported emancipation because it was "right in itself" and would destroy "an odious and dangerous aristocracy."

With the war over, Johnson told returning black troops that they must "prove" themselves "competent for the rights that the government has guaranteed [them]," expressed hope the two races could live harmoniously in an "experiment" in freedom, and warned that if the experiment failed, the solution might lie in removing Negroes from the United States. Negroes doubtless sensed the implicit threat in view of the fact that newspapers were already quoting the President as having said: "This is a country for white men, and by G-d, so long as I am President, it shall be a government for white men."

Any lingering doubt as to his attitude was dispelled by his message to Congress in December, 1867. Negroes, he said, had "shown less capacity for government than any other race of people. No independent government of any form has ever been successful in their hands. On the contrary, wherever they have been left to their own devices, they have shown a constant tendency to relapse into barbarism." Granting suffrage to black men, he continued, would endanger the rights of property, put the white man at the mercy of the Negro, destroy the South economically,

---

[2] Kenneth M. Stampp, *The Era of Reconstruction, 1865–1877* (New York: Alfred A. Knopf, Inc., 1965), p. 54.

and fasten upon that section "such a tyranny as this continent has never yet witnessed."

Like most of his fellow Americans, Andrew Johnson was little equipped to deal sympathetically with black people as human beings. Thus, he—and they—were ill-prepared to meet in statesmanlike fashion the central problem of the Reconstruction era: the role of the Negro in American society.

To understand something of the nature of that problem we must look at the position of the American Negro in the 1860's.

Of the 31,513,000 people living in the United States in 1860, 4,441,000, nearly 14 per cent of the total, were classified by the U.S. Census as Negroes. The great mass of these—4,097,000—were in the South; 3,838,000 were slaves, and among them were 411,000 mulattoes. Throughout the nation there were 488,000 free Negroes, of whom more than a third bore the marks of white ancestry. Most free Negroes— 258,000—lived in the South.

"Free people of color" were welcome in few places. In the North they were almost universally segregated, excluded from public life, and their children barred from white public schools. In those areas where separate Negro schools were provided they were inadequately financed and instruction was poor. In the South free Negroes were viewed as potentially dangerous to slavery; they were "kept in their place" by stringent legislation, hostile public officials, and the dread of re-enslavement—a dread given substance by actions of several states providing for actual re-enslavement of free Negroes.

Most, whether in North or South, lived in or near towns, where employment opportunities were most favorable. Many led marginal existences as domestics, longshoremen, odd-job laborers, and the like. Others, however, were professional people, skilled workmen, shopkeepers, farmers, and planters. Of these, a considerable number accumulated property. In Virginia, for example, free Negroes owned 60,000 acres of farm land in 1860. In North Carolina, they possessed nearly a million dollars in real estate and personal property. New York Negro business men had $755,000 invested in their own enterprises.

In that city, as well as in others such as Charleston, New Orleans, and Cincinnati there were enclaves of wealthy and cultured Negroes, who, except for color, were almost indistinguishable from their white counterparts. They carried on the same kind of social life, believed in the virtues of their section, and, in the South, held slaves. After the war, however, many men from this group became active in the cause of the freedman. Dr. J. T. Roudanez, for example, a New Orleans physician, spent much of his fortune subsidizing the New Orleans *Tribune,* an aggressive spokesman for the black man during Reconstruction.

No matter what their occupation, free Negroes were objects of white resentment, especially when employment opportunities were limited. In East Coast cities Irish dockers rioted against hiring of Negro long-shoremen. Elsewhere, particularly in the South, whites rioted, petitioned, and legislated to eliminate competition from black physicians, carpenters, plasterers, and other skilled and professional workers.

Among free Negroes there was a small but significant intellectual community. It included such figures as Frederick Douglass; James Mc-Cune Smith, physician, graduate of the University of Glasgow, who in 1846 published a paper on the influence of climate on longevity; William C. Nell, who researched the role of the Negro in the Revolutionary War; J. W. C. Pennington, recipient of a Doctor of Divinity degree from the University of Heidelberg and author of an early work (1841) on Negro history; and Martin R. Delany, product of the Harvard Medical School who later became prominent in Reconstruction politics in South Carolina. Their numbers would soon be swelled by Negroes studying at Oberlin, Franklin, and Rutland colleges and at Harvard Medical School.

Most black men, of course, were slaves, and most of these were field hands: planting, hoeing, harvesting corn and cotton. But this does not mean they were the ignorant barbarians they have been so often described. Southern agriculture was not noted for its efficiency, but field hands were well trained in its techniques and in effect were skilled laborers—a fact brought home to white planters when they tried to substitute foreign for Negro labor in the post-war years. Among the field hands there was a small class of "drivers"—men who actually supervised work in the fields. Often the lash that fell on black backs was wielded by black hands.

Among the slaves there was also a significant number of skilled craftsmen: carpenters, weavers, blacksmiths, coopers, boot and shoemakers. Their skills were such that owners often leased their services to contractors in towns and cities; indeed, a considerable number of such slaves lived permanently in the towns. Since such slaves often displaced white men, white bitterness naturally followed.

House servants comprised a small, privileged group: on the whole, they were well fed, well clothed, well taken care of. Many learned to read and write, despite its being unlawful. In daily contact with their masters, they tended to identify themselves with the masters and to look down on field hands—and poor whites. In turn, field hands regarded house servants with distrust, for they had a reputation for betraying escape and insurrection plans. And yet, as Joel Williamson notes, when Union armies entered South Carolina, house servants defected even before the field hands! [3]

The war itself, even before formal emancipation, forced people in both the Union and the Confederacy to reconsider the place and role of the Negro, albeit reluctantly and grudgingly.

In the Confederacy, the war was marked by the steady erosion of slavery. Lacking a market, cotton piled up on the plantations. Slaves, once an undeniable asset, were now a grievous liability. Some planters encouraged the Negroes to grow their own food and to sell surplus produce where possible; craftsmen were leased out in greater numbers. Some planters, unable to bear the burden of idle slaves, turned them out to fend for themselves. Even those who could afford to maintain slaves found the expense of moving them hither and yon in face of advancing Union armies almost insupportable. Slave prices declined sharply.

Leading Confederate figures, such as Judah P. Benjamin, the secretary of state, and J. L. Alcorn, a leading planter-politician of Mississippi, began to talk of emancipation. Responding to the new situation, Negro behavior changed. Despite a fresh wave of restrictive legislation and the organization of "home guards" to protect apprehensive whites against expected insurrections, Negroes became increasingly "impudent" and "insolent"—according to white reports—and in Mississippi and South Carolina staged minor uprisings. Most slaves, however, continued to work faithfully—until the Union armies neared. Then they "voted with their feet," swarming into the federal lines in such numbers as to impede military operations and to create grave problems of supply and morale. They also furnished the invaders with invaluable military intelligence and significant service as spies and scouts.

Eventually, under pressure from Robert E. Lee and other Confederate generals, the Confederate Congress in February, 1865, provided for incorporation of slaves into the army, on the understanding that such slaves would be free after the war. In a last-minute bid for foreign recognition, the Confederacy even pledged emancipation. Both measures came too late to affect the course of the war, but their significance was not lost upon either whites or blacks. The "peculiar institution" was no longer viable but it was not so clear what the new role of the Negro was to be.

In the North, public opinion and government alike were less than

[3] Joel Williamson, *After Slavery: The Negro in South Carolina During Reconstruction, 1861–1877* (Chapel Hill: University of North Carolina Press, 1965), p. 34.

enthusiastic about Negro participation in the war. Although the Navy early adopted a policy of permitting Negro enlistment, the army rejected Negro pleas for military service and efforts of free Negroes to form military units at their own expense were discouraged by state and local officials. Pressure from abolitionists and urgent local military necessities finally led to the formation of Negro units in South Carolina, Louisiana, and Tennessee during 1862, and in July of that year the Second Confiscation Act gave the President discretionary authority to enlist Negroes. Not until 1863, however, was it made national policy to use Negro troops—a development in which both the logic of emancipation and widespread white resistance to the draft played their parts.

By the end of the war at least 180,000 Negroes from all parts of the nation—including many impressed refugees—had served in the army. They served not only in garrison and service outfits, but also in combat units. They were segregated and discriminated against. For a long time their pay was substantially less than that of white soldiers, they were denied bounties paid to whites, their families shared little in the financial aid extended to soldiers' families by the states, and capable Negroes found it almost impossible to become officers. Only about a hundred received commissions.

Black troops did not bear these indignities meekly. The famous Fifty-fourth and Fifty-fifth Massachusetts Regiments, distinguished for valor, went without pay for 18 months rather than accept the discriminatory rate. Before Congress finally remedied the grievance in 1864 the men had become openly rebellious. A minor mutiny over the issue did take place in a South Carolina regiment.

Nevertheless, Negro soldiers compiled a distinguished record. In relation to their numbers, they had fewer desertions than their white comrades—and many more casualties. More than a third of those enrolled were dead or missing by the war's end—nearly double the rate for the army as a whole. Most were victims of wounds and disease. Combat troops took part in 200 engagements, 39 of which were classified as major. Some of the latter were among the bloodiest of the war: Milliken's Bend, Fort Wagner, Fort Pillow (scene of the notorious Confederate massacre of Negro troops who had surrendered), and the last, long campaign in Virginia. One two-day battle in that campaign brought 37 Congressional Medals of Honor to the troops—14 went to Negro soldiers. By the end of the war, many Union commanders who had doubted the combat effectiveness of colored troops were ready to agree with General Grant in his comment after the successful campaign for control of the Mississippi in 1863: "All that have been tried [in combat] have fought bravely."

Unfortunately, the black war record was soon lost to view. For generations to come the myth persisted that Negroes lacked courage in warfare. Even today many history books ignore the Negro's role in actively fighting for his freedom. As a result, many Negro Americans have little knowledge of the part their ancestors played in winning them freedom and liberating American democracy from the incubus of slavery.

If the Federal Government had been reluctant to accept Negro soldiers, it was equally unwilling to face up to the problem of slavery. Committed to the doctrine that the war was waged solely to preserve the Union, believing that the war was going to be short and that it could not be won without the support of the slave-holding Border States and of anti-Negro Northerners (who found vent for their prejudices in riots against Negroes in many Northern cities), the Lincoln Administration sought to avoid the explosive issue of abolition. Consequently, it neglected to provide the army commanders with a uniform policy to follow when they entered slave territory.

For them, it was a problem which could not be avoided; every incursion into the South brought fugitive slaves within Union lines. What was to be done with them? Lacking direction from Washington, each general used his own judgment. Some, like Benjamin F. Butler in Virginia, declared the blacks "contraband of war" and put them to work on army projects. Others, like Henry W. Halleck in the West, ordered fugitives returned to their masters. Two, John C. Fremont in Missouri and David Hunter in South Carolina, provided for emancipation—and were countermanded by Lincoln.

Congress grappled with the problem, but no decisive action was taken for nearly a year. Finally, in March, 1862, it forbade the army to return fugitives, and in July declared free the slaves of active Confederates. Like the later Emancipation Proclamation the law freed few slaves, but it did foreshadow a new status for black men—in the future. But what was to be done about the immediate problem of the thousands of slaves trekking along with Union armies?

Again there was little guidance or aid from Washington. Philanthropic and religious organizations tried to fill the gap, but their resources were limited and often wasted in internecine quarrels. At best they could touch only the surface of the problem: there were tens of thousands of refugees huddled in camps where food and shelter were scarce, disease rampant, mortality frightful, and the behavior of the soldiers generally hostile. Only the government could cope with such a problem, and lacking a clear-cut government policy, each commander was on his own. Some, taking the easiest way out, permitted white lessees of abandoned plantations to employ Negroes on contract—a plan made to order for unscrupulous employers, of whom there seemed to be no wartime scarcity. James Yeatman, reporting to the Western Sanitary Commission after an investigation in 1863, said the Negroes "do not realize they are free men. They say they are told they are, but then they are taken and hired out to men who treat them, so far as providing for them is concerned, far worse than their 'secesh' masters did."

There were other generals, however, who displayed uncommon insight into the immediate and long-range problems of the freedmen. Rufus Saxton in the Sea Islands of South Carolina and U. S. Grant at Davis Bend, Mississippi, established colonies in which Negroes were allotted Confederate lands (which the freedmen believed were to be their own) and given autonomy in the management of their economic and political life. The results were impressive. Despite the problems which afflict all agricultural enterprise—insect pests, uncertain weather, inadequate capital—the former slaves proved not only financially successful but also politically capable.

Unfortunately, the significance of these experiments was lost on the country at large. Treasury officials moved in on the Sea Islands, claiming jurisdiction over abandoned plantations on grounds of unpaid federal taxes. They by-passed Saxton's attempts to keep the land in the hands of the freedmen, set terms of sale so that individual Negroes could not compete at the auctions, and eventually sold most of the good land to whites—meaning, in this instance, Northern speculators. This took place during the Lincoln Administration. The Johnson Administration ended the Davis Bend project when presidential pardon restored the lands to their Confederate owners.

Despite these disappointments, few freedmen returned to their old masters. In the words of John Eaton, Grant's remarkable Superintendent of Freedmen, "Discouraged, panic-stricken, suspicious they were; but ready to exchange their hard-won and unhappy freedom for the sometimes easier conditions of slavery, they were not."

That "unhappy freedom" was to last long beyond the war, but the conditions which prompted Eaton's characterization finally brought action from Congress. In March, 1865, it passed an act assuming federal responsibility for the care of freedmen and destitute white refugees for the duration of the war and one year thereafter. To administer the measure it established a Bureau for the Relief of Freedmen and Refugees in the War Department and authorized the issuance of food, clothing, and fuel for immediate relief of distress.

Of greater long-term significance was a section relating to land distribution which gave good ground for the general belief of Negroes that after the war the Federal Government was going to allocate lands to them in forty-acre lots. Since that belief has been often adduced as proof of Negro gullibility and the significance of the section glossed over in discussions of Reconstruction, it is essential to quote it at some length:

> . . . the commissioner [of the Freedmen's Bureau], under the direction of the President, shall have authority to set apart, for the use of loyal refugees and freedmen, such tracts of land within the insurrectionary states as shall have been abandoned, or to which the United States shall have acquired title by confiscation or sale, or otherwise, and to every male citizen, whether refugeee or freedman, . . . *there shall be assigned not more than forty acres of such land,* and the person to whom it was so assigned shall be protected in the use and enjoyment of the land for the term of three years. . . . At the end of said term, or at any time during said term, the occupants of any parcels so assigned *may purchase* the land and receive such title thereto as the United States can convey, . . . (Italics supplied).

Careful examination of the wording, as LaWanda Cox has suggested, reveals that the act guaranteed no permanent title to Negroes who might acquire land, for "any title the United States might obtain to rebel lands would be limited, in accordance with the Joint Resolution accompanying the Confiscation Act of 1862, to the lifetime of Southern owners." [4] Nevertheless, it is understandable why Negroes felt they had a firm pledge from the United States Government to help them acquire land.

The situation of the black American when the war ended was ambiguous. As soldier and civilian he had contributed significantly to saving the Union and winning his own freedom, and by some Northerners this was duly appreciated. Yet in neither section was the freedman welcome.

Northerners as a whole, willing to concede freedom, were hostile to equality. Many of them dreaded an incursion of black folk after the war —especially among lower paid workers who feared Negro competition and some not so poorly paid who resented possible Negro entry into their crafts. The use of Negroes as strikebreakers during the war and their employment in areas where whites were out of work resulted in agitation and riots and intensified anti-Negro feeling.

Such sentiment, however, was by no means confined to workingmen. Between 1865 and 1867 voters in Connecticut, Wisconsin, and Ohio rejected proposals for Negro suffrage; in 1868 only 8 out of 16 Northern

[4] LaWanda Cox, "The Promise of Land for the Freedmen," *Mississippi Valley Historical Review,* XLV, No. 3 (1958), 419.

states permitted Negroes to vote. Oregon even continued its pre-war prohibition against the entry of free Negroes: the long-dead law was finally repealed in 1926!

In the South, the black man was the living, ever-present symbol of defeat. In addition, he was now viewed as a menace to the genetic purity of the Anglo-Saxon "race"—an interesting psychological development in view of the large number of mulattoes among both slave and free Negroes.

Outside of his own strength, as yet largely unorganized and inarticulate, all that the Negro could rely upon was the word of the Congress of the United States, promising him land, and ironically, that of Andrew Johnson, who had told them in October, 1864, "I will indeed be your Moses . . . and lead you to a fairer future of liberty and peace," in a speech which called for the break-up of large plantations and distribution of the land among "free, industrious and honest farmers."

As President, concerned with restoring the Union and frustrating the "money power" of New England, Johnson had other views. He would offer the white South such generous terms that in effect the process of "restoration" would be voluntary: he would, he said, "only take the initiatory steps to enable them to do the things which it was incumbent upon them to perform." Thus, he hoped, before Congress met again in December, 1865, the Union would be restored—and he would have asserted the authority of the presidency, thwarted the Radical Republicans (with whom he had broken after a warm but brief courtship), and staked out the ground for a party of the center which would help insure his election in 1868.

To that end, he extended a general amnesty to Confederates; those excepted from the amnesty, such as planters owning $20,000 or more in taxable property, were eligible for special pardons, which were freely granted in the summer and fall of 1865. Accompanying amnesty was his prescription for Reconstruction. He would appoint in each Southern state a provisional governor who would in turn call a convention to make necessary constitutional changes and supervise the election of delegates. Voting and office-holding would be restricted to those who had taken the amnesty oath and who qualified under the state election laws of 1860. This latter provision, of course, effectively excluded Negroes from political life, and was accordingly denounced by Negroes, like those of Vicksburg, Mississippi, as "unjust" and "damaging" to peaceful relations between the races.

The convention would establish voting and office-holding requirements for regular elections thereafter for state and federal offices. In the interim period the provisional governor would continue in office existing officials who had taken the loyalty oath; in cases where they had not, new appointments would be made. In private communications Johnson emphasized that the states must also invalidate their ordinances of secession, ratify the Thirteenth Amendment abolishing slavery, and repudiate Confederate war debts. Apart from these, he made no demands on the South—he had no wish, he said, to "irritate or humiliate the people of the South."

Johnson's plan might well have carried. Its very moderation appealed to the mass of Northern voters who cared little for the Negro traditionally elected moderate candidates, and wanted nothing better than to deal with their current problems and make the most of the opportunities opening up in the post-war period. Not least of these was the prospect of exploiting the resources of Southern coal, iron, and timber. Swift and painless restoration of the Union, with its promise of a peaceful and cooperative South, would not only restore the old national market but also open up a new era of profitable expansion. Thus, in the summer and fall of 1865, Johnson enjoyed overwhelming support in the North among both Republicans and Democrats. In the South, his popularity was enhanced by the endorsement given him by Robert E. Lee. Yet his plan miscarried. Why?

In the first place, in breaking with the Radicals early in his administration, Johnson no doubt strengthened himself with the moderates; he also brought into active opposition such redoubtable figures as Ben Wade of Ohio, Zachariah Chandler of Michigan, Charles Sumner of Massachusetts, and Thaddeus Stevens of Pennsylvania, men who could be as grim and inflexible as Johnson himself on matters of principle. They were as much at home in internal Republican politics as Johnson was awkward. Operating from strong power bases in their home districts, they were generally sure of re-election, and thus, through the operation of seniority, well represented on major committees. In addition, their continuous service in the House and the Senate gave them an assurance and authority which was not without its influence on younger members. Indeed, there was some feeling that they represented the rank and file opinion of the party better than moderates and conservatives, who, coming usually from marginal districts, had to cater to Democrats and conservatives to win the votes necessary for election.

True, the Radicals were a minority, a minority hard to define because they differed among themselves on almost every major issue, including that of the place of the Negro in American society. They were, however, agreed on abolition, thorough reorganization of Southern society to bring it into line with the free enterprise North, and maintenance of Republican ascendancy in the Federal Government. The last was the indispensable condition of the other two. Indeed, it was also indispensable for the preservation of the Union itself, for Radicals came to believe that treason itself, in the person of Johnson, sat in "the Presidential chair." And it was indispensable because only through the Republican party could their various interests be reconciled and promoted.

Yet this ascendancy was threatened by the Johnson program, which permitted, if indeed it did not encourage, revival of the Democratic party in the South. When Southern Democrats reunited with their Northern brethren they could easily outvote the sectional, minority Republican party. Clearly perceiving the danger, Radicals formed a cohesive and influential bloc of resistance to the President, around which gradually coalesced moderate and conservative elements increasingly alienated by the White House.

This alienation had its origins among men who approved much of the substance of the President's policy but denied his authority to act. They were among the Republicans who, in enacting the Wade-Davis bill in 1864, despite Lincoln's opposition, had flatly asserted that Reconstruction was the prerogative of Congress, not of the President. Lincoln had pocket-vetoed the bill, but he had not changed the opinions of the men who backed it. William Pitt Fessenden, for example, the prestigious moderate Senator from Maine, supported Johnson, but he had not given up his belief "that the question of reconstruction . . . should properly be settled by Congress, and can not be settled by any other power but Congress in any possible way." It is significant that when Congress met in December, 1865, the Radical plan to establish a Joint Committee on Reconstruction on such terms as to make Reconstruction exclusively a Congressional function passed both houses with moderate and even conservative support, and that when the committee was formed it was dominated by moderates.

Johnson's plan miscarried also because it had no place for the Negro as citizen. Despite pressure from Radicals and protests from Negroes that they could not "understand the justice of denying the elective franchise to men who have been fighting for their country, while it is freely given to men who have just returned from four years of fighting against it," the President was adamant. He would not interfere with the Southern states, then engaged in barring the Negro from the ballot. This meant, as Republicans were quick to realize, that the South— meaning Democrats—would return to the Union with an actual *increase* in representation.

Under slavery, the Constitution allowed only three-fifths of the slave population to be counted for purposes of representation. Now, with abolition, the entire Negro population would be used as a base. According to Thaddeus Stevens, this would result in an increase of seventeen in the Southern Congressional delegation. The danger to their party in such an eventuality needed no elaboration to Republicans; increasing numbers of them came to agree with the Radicals that safety lay in Negro—meaning Republican—suffrage in the South.

Johnson, sensing the drift of opinion, in August, 1865, counselled Governor William L. Sharkey of Mississippi to frustrate the Radicals by extending the franchise to literate and property-owning Negroes. Sharkey, a Johnson appointee, ignored the advice, and the President took no further action—either in Mississippi or elsewhere. Thus, Johnson lost the support of the Negroes, many of whom had apparently hoped that he would follow, in the words of North Carolina Negroes, the policies of "our murdered friend and father," Lincoln, forced them to look elsewhere for leadership—and at the same time helped promote the coalition of moderates and Radical Republicans concerned about the fate of their party.

Even so, Johnson might still have salvaged his policy. After all, few Northern farmers or mechanics lost sleep over Negro rights; Republican politicians might identify the threat to their party with a threat to the nation, but many voters were skeptical; indeed, most voters, anxious for a return to the ways of peace, were inclined to give the President the benefit of any doubt which might arise. In addition, Johnson enjoyed the support of powerful newspapers, such as the New York *Tribune,* New York *Herald,* New York *Times,* and the Chicago *Tribune;* the business press; white organized labor; and leading public figures such as Henry Ward Beecher, the most popular preacher of the day, and Governor John Andrew of Massachusetts, Senators William Pitt Fessenden of Maine and Lyman Trumbull of Illinois.

Active Democrats saw in Johnson one of their own, and Republicans united behind him because they realized the necessity of party unity. Thus, they were willing to go along, however reluctantly, with the President's "restoration" program. Besides, in their view, the program was an "experiment"—to be modified or abandoned when experience had shown its inadequacy. The concensus broke down when the "experiment" did indeed prove a failure, in the Republican view, and Johnson refused to abandon it.

The President's problems arose from a series of developments in the South which in turn grew out of his inability to appreciate the realities of the Southern power structure. As we have seen, Johnson's belief in the virtues of the yeomanry led him to conclude that once freed of planter domination they would create democratic governments of their own.

In fact, the yeomanry, lacking its own leadership, and still imbued with traditional respect for aristocracy, turned back to their old leaders —following, ironically, an example set by Johnson himself, when he had appointed as provisional governors such men as Sharkey of Mississippi, who had been a slave-owner and a Chief Justice, and Benjamin F. Perry of South Carolina, who had been a Confederate judge. Nearly every Johnson government fell into the hands of planters and Confederates. Confronted with the reality, Johnson abandoned his scheme of confiscation and distribution of confiscated lands among yeoman farmers. Naturally, Southern Unionists who looked for some reward for patriotic service and others who looked toward a new day for the South were antagonized.

This was far from being the most significant consequence of the Johnson policy in the South. More important were its effects on the Southern mood and politics. At the end of the war the Confederate South fully expected the Union to impose rigorous conditions for restoration, and white Southerners generally were prepared to follow the leaders who urged accommodation to the expected demands. The logic of defeat seemed plain: the South would have "to propitiate the powers at Washington."

When it became apparent that there was going to be no coercion, that Johnson was not going to drive a hard bargain (such as insisting upon restricted Negro suffrage), and that he was going to give the Southern states complete freedom once they had complied with his formula for restoration, the situation changed. The self-styled "men of good sense" found themselves vulnerable to attacks from those who sought to resume the struggle with the Black Republicans; the mood of cooperation slipped into one of militancy; and the process of accommodation became transformed into testing the limits to which the white South could safely assert its new found power.

The testing went too far. Misled by Johnson's assurances that his Northern opposition came only from disgruntled Radicals, encouraged by his tacit acquiescence in many of their actions, deluded by their belief that with resurgent Democracy on the way the Republican party was doomed to extinction, and miscalculating the impact of their words and deeds on Northern opinion, white Southerners followed a course which brought down on them and the President the very fate they sought to avoid. As Gideon Welles, Johnson's Secretary of the Navy and loyal follower, noted at the time, "The entire South seem to be stupid and vindictive, know not their friends, and pursuing just the course which their opponents, the Radicals, desire." What was that course?

It was increasingly a course of militancy, expressed first in words—editorials, sermons, speeches—setting forth the mood in a variety of opinions. The South was in the hands of godless men. Negroes should be deported and their places taken by docile Chinese. The Confederacy might yet be revived. Just enough concessions should be made to the North to keep native whites in power while they restored the old order. Through such means the South would become the balance of power by 1868, and then, in the words of James H. Campbell of South Carolina, "we will have our own way."

Some of the words had more impact than others, of course. Among these were suggestions that the national debt incurred for waging the war might be repudiated. "I am opposed," said a Virginia candidate for Congress in 1865, "to the Southern states being taxed at all for the redemption of this national debt, either directly or indirectly; and I will vote to repeal all laws that have heretofore been passed for that purpose." He predicted that once Southern members were seated in Congress they would attempt either to repudiate the national debt, or assume the Confederate debt, or provide compensation for emancipation—or all three.

Such proposals may not have had the endorsement of "men of good sense," but they could hardly fail to arouse apprehension among the thousands of Northerners who had invested in war bonds during Jay Cooke's hard-sell campaigns. Repudiation played a significant part not only in Republican propaganda but also in the private correspondence of Republicans in the period. They took the threat with utter seriousness.

If bondholders were aroused, so also were Northern businessmen who poured into the South after the war to take advantage of Southern poverty in acquiring plantations and lands bearing coal, iron, and timber. While some succeeded, many others felt the keen edge of Southern white hostility. Southerners did not like Yankee ways and did not want them as neighbors; they resented the advantage which the Yankee took of their plight; and they were disturbed by the Yankee practice of paying for labor, including Negro labor, in wages—a threat to the established pattern of racial paternalism. To them, the Northern businessman was the Yankee conqueror in his most obvious form—money-grubbing, unscrupulous, subversive of the Southern way of life. To paraphrase E. Merton Coulter, the distinguished interpreter of the traditional South in our day, would the white South sell out?

The Southern answer was No. Too weak to resist openly the Northern business invasion, they responded with social ostracism and in some cases, with violence. The New York *Herald*, a strong supporter of Johnson, reported from Georgia that the armed bands preying on Negroes did not confine themselves to blacks: "The 'regulators' go to the bottom of the matter, and strive to make it uncomfortably warm for any new settler with demoralizing innovations of wages for 'niggers'." An agent sent by the New York State Chamber of Commerce to investigate opportunities in the South reported that the Southern "temper of hatred for the Northern people" made it difficult "to live and safely transact business in any section of the South." Businessmen naturally turned to Congress for relief. As Roscoe Conkling, a member of the House at the time, later recalled to the Supreme Court, "complaints of oppression in respect of property and other rights made by citizens of the North who had settled in the South were rife in and out of Congress." Since businessmen had no need to convince Radicals, they exerted their pressure on moderates and conservatives.

The behavior of the constitutional conventions which met under the Johnson program did little to abate rising Northern feeling. South Carolina refused to fly the Stars and Stripes over the convention hall. Mississippi flatly refused to ratify the Thirteenth Amendment. These two states did not repudiate their Confederate debts; Georgia and North Carolina did so only under strong presidential pressure. Some conventions, declining to concede the illegality of secession, repealed rather than repudiated their ordinances of secession. Georgia, in agreeing to abolition, coupled it with a demand for compensation.

The new state constitutions, while conceding abolition, established no rights for the freedmen as citizens, restricted voting, office-holding, and public schools to whites. Indeed, the tone of the conventions generally was symbolized in the message to the South Carolina convention from the provisional governor, Benjamin F. Perry, "this is a white man's government, and intended for white men only."

In the elections which followed, it became apparent that by "white men's government" the voters understood this to mean planters and ex-Confederates, including among the latter representatives of the small farmers and poor whites of the hills who were considerably less flexible on the race issue and on dealing with the North than were the planters.

Every state, with the exception of Tennessee, fell under the control of these groups. To Congress the voters sent seventy-four Confederates, including former generals, colonels, cabinet members, Congressmen, and state legislators; Georgia even sent to the Senate Alexander H. Stephens, the Confederate vice-president, then on parole on a charge of treason. Many of the new office-holders were legally ineligible under the act of July 2, 1862, requiring an "iron-clad oath" of every elected or appointed official that he had never voluntarily given aid or comfort to the Confederacy. Some were also among classes excluded from presidential amnesty and not yet pardoned. Johnson sought to break at least part of the impasse through liberal use of the pardoning power.

Southerners might rejoice, as did many of their newspaper editors, that all this boded well for the President. Increasing numbers of Northerners would have agreed rather with Johnson's Governor of North Carolina, William W. Holden, who reported to the President in December, 1865: "I regret to say there is much of a rebellious spirit still in this state. . . . In May and June last these rebellious spirits would not have dared to show their heads . . . but leniency has emboldened them, and the Copperhead now shows his fangs."

Northern feelings were further stirred when news came of the Black Codes passed by Southern legislatures during 1865 and early 1866.

In the closing months of the war and for some time thereafter innumerable Negroes left the plantations on which they had worked, sought work elsewhere on better terms, or congregated in the towns. This wandering was interpreted by the whites as proof of what they had long contended: Negroes would not work without compulsion and could not work without white supervision. The fact was, of course, that the white Southerner was face to face with a new phenomenon—Negro mobility—and it is not surprising that he, like others faced with situations at once new and frightening, fell back on old clichés to comfort himself and rationalize his behavior. The mobility of the Negro had more realistic origins.

Of prime importance was Negro knowledge, however imperfect it may have been, of the language of the Freedmen's Bureau Act which we have already noted. The promise of the Act was reinforced by the speeches of Thaddeus Stevens and other Congressmen advocating confiscation of the estates of leading Confederates and distribution of the land to adult male freedmen. Furthermore, many were aware of the famous Field Order No. 15 of General William T. Sherman, issued in January, 1865. This allotted to Negroes the Sea Islands south of Charleston, South Carolina, and rice plantations on the rivers as far as 30 miles inland. The 40,000 freedmen who took possession of 485,000 acres firmly—and mistakenly—believed they had good legal title. To others it was a token of what was to come, probably as early as New Year's Day, 1866. Under these circumstances it is no wonder that Negroes refused to commit themselves to long term labor contracts.

Negro reluctance to work under contract also is to be explained on other grounds. Terms imposed by many planters smacked too much of slavery to be acceptable: the work was hard, the hours long, sickness common. In many cases the Negroes went unpaid—and in addition were subjected to the beatings and floggings associated with slavery. In some areas planters agreed among themselves to keep wages down and to rent or sell no land to freedmen, which resulted in freedmen moving to cities and towns to work in mines and on railroads where pay and conditions were better. Some Negroes were not voluntary wanderers at all: new legislation in some states closed to them occupations in which they were skilled, and some planters, turning from cotton to cereal production, turned Negroes off the land to fend for themselves. Still others were on the move for a simple human reason: they wanted to find missing parents, children, husbands, wives.

Given the racial mythology to which white Southerners had been conditioned for generations, it is not difficult to understand why they reacted strongly to Negro freedom and the Negro aspiration for land. Both presented clear and present dangers to the Southern way of life; as U. B. Phillips, the famous Southern historian, pointed out, the resolve of the white South to keep it a "white man's country" has been the "central theme of Southern history." For that purpose, the Negro must be kept in subordination. The Black Codes were a means to that end, although they were usually justified as an attempt to deal with the problems of labor supply, vice, crime, and other social problems attendant upon the sudden emergence into freedom of nearly four million slaves.

It is difficult to summarize the codes, for they varied from state to state—and North Carolina passed none. In general they recognized the new status of the Negro by extending to him such long established white rights as legal marriage, ownership of property, entrance into contracts, to sue and be sued (with some limitations relative to suing of white men). Beyond that, the Negro was placed in a special—that is, inferior—position.

In South Carolina only a magistrate could order arrest of a white man accused of crime against a Negro but any white could arrest a Negro "upon view of a misdemeanor." Black "orphans"—youngsters without parents or whose parents could not take care of them—were subject to compulsory "apprenticeship" to white masters, who had the right to whip "moderately" those under 18; older "apprentices" could be whipped with judicial approval. Labor contract details between "servants" and "masters" were spelled out. When wages could not be agreed upon, they were set by a local white judge. A Negro failing to enter into such a contract was guilty of a misdemeanor, subject to punishment.

Skilled mechanics and artisans were effectively barred from pursuing their vocations on their own by requiring special licenses, costing ten dollars a year (at a time when the yearly wage of farm labor in the state was $100). These licenses, issued by judges after examination of applicants' moral character and proficiency, were revocable on complaint. "Vagrancy" was defined so broadly as to cover all Negro unemployed; so-called "vagrants" were subject to terms at hard labor for public authorities or for private masters. This provision, common to many codes, in effect compelled a Negro to remain under unsatisfactory conditions lest he be punished as a vagrant for leaving.

Mississippi, while incorporating in its code many provisions similar to those of South Carolina, contained unique features which particularly exasperated the North. A special tax was levied on Negroes to take care of their own poor and infirm; Negroes who failed to pay the tax were *ipso facto* guilty of "vagrancy" and subject to hiring out to private masters. As Vernon L. Wharton pointed out, this represented a new departure in American legislation.[5] Another section prohibited Negroes from renting or leasing land outside of towns—a provision designed not only to provide an adequate labor supply for planters and farmers but also to prevent the growth of independent Negro farmers. To make certain that no loopholes remained, the legislature enacted that "all penal and criminal laws now in force . . . defining offenses and describing the mode of punishment of crimes and misdemeanors *committed by slaves*, free negroes, or mulattoes, . . . are hereby *reenacted*, and decreed to be in full force and effect, against *freedmen*, free negroes and mulattoes, . . ." (Italics supplied.) In short, the old slave code was restored.

In addition to the codes, local ordinances strictly regulated the hours and conditions under which Negroes could live or travel in towns and villages. A Negro who lived under them testified that they "virtually re-enslaved those that had been emancipated."

Southern Negroes responded to the codes with demands for their repeal, reflecting in their language both the Negro's new sense of dignity and his determination to have a voice in shaping his destiny. For example, a state convention of South Carolina Negroes, reminding whites that Negroes might well ask for "special favor and encouragement, on the principle that the strong should aid the weak," went on to say, "We ask for no special privileges, . . . We ask only for *even handed justice*, for the removal of such positive obstructions and dis-

---

[5] Vernon Lane Wharton, *The Negro in Mississippi, 1865–1890* (New York: Harper & Row, Publishers, Inc., 1965), p. 86.

abilities as past and recent legislation has thrown in our way." Listing such discriminations, the petition emphasized the Negroes' understanding of their new status: "We simply ask that we shall be recognized as *men*; . . . that . . . we shall be dealt with as others are—in equity and justice." (Italics in original). Similar messages came from Negro meetings in Georgia and Alabama. These were widely reprinted in the North.

The moderation of language characteristic of the Negro petitions was conspicuously lacking in Northern press comment. The New York *Tribune* charged South Carolina with trying to re-establish slavery; the New York *Times* termed that state's code, "bloody." The Chicago *Tribune* threatened that the "men of the North" would turn Mississippi "into a frog pond before they will allow such laws to disgrace one foot of soil . . . over which the flag of freedom waves." That all these newspapers were in some measure supporters of Johnson gives some indication of Northern reaction to the codes. At this point the President apparently felt it wise to yield to the storm of protest. When military commanders nullified in part the Mississippi and South Carolina codes he failed to countermand them, although he assured a Mississippi delegation that only the courts should nullify the laws.

The growing feeling in the North that the freedman could not safely be trusted to the care of the South was further stimulated by almost daily reports of anti-Negro violence in Southern states. These reports were given substance in widely reported hearings of the Joint Committee on Reconstruction early in 1866. Clara Barton, the famous Civil War nurse, furnished a gruesome personal account of a young Negro woman who had been flogged. Major General George A. Custer reported from Texas that murder of freedmen was "of weekly, if not daily occurrence." A Freedmen's Bureau agent recounted how armed white bands were "hunting, flogging, and killing colored people." William L. Sharkey, Johnson's provisional governor in Mississippi in 1865, attributed the violence to the Freedmen's Bureau and to the presence of colored troops. In any case, he said, because of disease and other factors, the Negro was "destined to extinction, beyond all doubt."

That some Southerners were willing to hasten the process seemed evident (to Northern opinion) in riots in Memphis and New Orleans in the summer of 1866. In the Tennessee city the local police, after a brawl with colored soldiers, terrorized the Negro community, killing 46 and wounding between 70 and 80 people. In New Orleans an attempt by Republicans to unseat the government of Confederates which took office in 1865 resulted in an attack by police and a white mob on Negro paraders and their white allies. Among the Republicans 48 were killed,

68 severely wounded and 98 slightly wounded. Their opponents counted one dead and ten injured—none seriously. As General Philip Sheridan reported to General Grant: "It was no riot: it was an absolute massacre by the police, . . . It was a murder which the mayor and police of this city perpetrated without the shadow of necessity."

The Memphis and New Orleans bloodshed not only caused revulsion in the North, which contributed to the resounding Republican success in the fall elections; it also helped discredit the President in the eyes of many moderates. Their disenchantment was expressed after the New Orleans riot by E. L. Godkin, editor of *The Nation*, one of the most influential weeklies in the country: "The coolness with which he refrained from expressing one word of honest indignation at the slaughter, in an American city, of unarmed men by a mob of their political opponents . . . is, perhaps, the most alarming incident in this sad affair."

The white South, then, contributed no little to undermining faith in the Johnson "experiment." Its words and actions also raised doubts among important sections of the Northern business community which drew them increasingly toward the Radicals, especially the Radical insistence on the need for continued Republican hegemony. Beyond the threats to the national debt and Southern hostility to Northern business, there were other questions:

If a reunited and strengthened Democratic party regained control of Congress, the White House, and eventually the Supreme Court, what would happen to the protective tariff, the outward, visible (and profitable) sign of the triumph of industrialism in national affairs? Southern Democrats, it was supposed, would naturally vote against it, as would most Northern Democrats. What would be the fate of the new national banking system and the generous federal subsidies for railroad building? Would the Democrats favor "sound money"? Was it not more likely that as spokesmen for disgruntled Western farmers and impoverished Southern planters they would choose the easy way of paper money and inflation? And how would Democrats, depending for much of their support on the urban workers, deal with the labor organizations taking hold in railroading, mining, and other industries? During the war some federal generals had forbidden strikes in their areas; in New York, Pennsylvania, Missouri, and Tennessee troops had been used to break strikes. Could Democrats be expected to do as much?

In other words, while individual elements of the business community might quarrel among themselves as to the direction of national policy (bankers, for example, favored "sound money," meaning contraction of the greenbacks in circulation, while debtor manufacturers endorsed inflation) each had a vital interest endangered by prospective Democratic victory, and thus each had a vital interest in maintaining Republican supremacy. The party had been the instrument of their triumph over Southern agrarianism; it must continue to be the instrument through which they could reconcile and promote their joint interests on this eve of unprecedented internal expansion.

Apprehension over a Democratic return to power was accentuated by distrust of Johnson's own economic philosophy and policies. He might have changed his attitude toward Southern planters, but he had modified his Jacksonian principles not a whit. Indeed, the destruction of the Southern aristocracy seemed to have sharpened his antagonism toward the Northern "aristocracy of the dollar," which, in his words, was striving to assume "that political control which the consolidation of great financial and political interest formerly gave to the slave oligarchy. . . . It is an aristocracy that can see in the people only a prey for extortion." Thus, in policy matters Johnson favored taxation of the wealthy, leaned toward inflation, opposed the protective tariff and the national banking system, asked Congress to halt the growth of railroad monopolies, and successfully blocked the sale of public lands in the West to private corporations, excoriating such sales as contrary to the public interest. Obviously, here was no man to promote the interests of business.

Northern business interests, then, faced eventual danger in Democratic control of the national government and immediate danger in the policies of Johnson. Salvation lay in maintaining Republican supremacy, even if that meant Negro suffrage in the South. The key to such supremacy lay in collaboration with the Radicals—but collaboration on business terms: no policy of confiscation, no land for the Negro, no disturbance of property relationships—only the minimum of political change required to assure Republican domination, i.e., Negro suffrage in the South to overbalance the white Democratic vote, which, of course, would be diminished through proscriptive legislation.

That group of Radicals, led by Sumner and Stevens, who were concerned with the long-range problem of integrating the Negro as free citizen in the American republic and saw land ownership as the means through which to assure the economic and political independence of the freedman, found such an offer of collaboration inadequate—but they had no alternative but to accept. As W. E. B. DuBois noted, "they accepted because they could not refuse." They could not refuse because they were aware of their own weakness in terms of practical politics: they were a minority even among Republicans, there was little hope that their policies would win Congressional approval, and what hope there might be rested in continued Republican control. They, too, were bound by the need for Republican supremacy in the national government.

Nevertheless, the developing alliance between business interests and Radicals does not of itself explain the eventual adoption of Negro suffrage in the South. Politics is a much more complex affair than the mere registering of economic influences; it has a logic of its own which transcends, even when it embodies, such interests. Reconstruction politics is an example of such logic in operation.

Republicans of all shades of opinion—conservative, moderate, radical —were convinced of the necessity of maintaining Republican supremacy. Such supremacy called for party unity. Radicals envisioned such unity as based on outright opposition to the President. The others, realizing Johnson's influence in the nation and indeed his following within the Republican party itself, believed that party unity must be based on harmonious relations with the White House.

Johnson, in what is usually described as a demonstration of political ineptitude but which equally well could have been an expression of distrust of Republicans as spokesmen for the "aristocracy of the dollar," destroyed the middle ground. He ended by uniting Republicans of all camps against him. The Reconstruction policy which followed was less the work of Sumner and Stevens than of moderates and conservatives such as Senators Lyman Trumbull of Illinois, John Sherman of Ohio, and William P. Fessenden of Maine, and Representatives John A. Bingham of Ohio and Elihu Washburne of Illinois.

Let us trace briefly how this came about.

When Congress met in December, 1865, Republicans were in a mood of disillusionment. The "experiment" had obviously failed: witness the Black Codes, election of Confederates to office, and the widespread violence against Unionists and Negroes in the South. It was thus possible for all those Republicans—Radicals, moderates, and conservatives— who believed that Reconstruction was essentially a Congressional function to unite behind Thaddeus Stevens' resolution establishing a Joint Committee on Reconstruction and barring Southern members of Congress until the committee's report had been heard and acted upon. While the resolution had been the work of Radicals, they did not dominate the committee which was appointed—despite his desire, Sumner was not even chosen a member! Power lay in the hands of such moderates as Fessenden, Trumbull, and Bingham. These men looked forward to collaboration with the President in a new program which would, in the words of Fessenden, be satisfactory "to the great bulk of Union men throughout the States."

The program consisted of three measures. First, expansion of the war-time Freedmen's Bureau not only to provide relief for Negroes and white refugees but also to protect the new status of the freedman by setting up courts to which he might repair for redress. This latter provision arose from the failure of local courts in the South to protect the freedmen—and indeed in some cases their use to keep the Negro in subjection. The Bureau courts were to function until such time as the states were restored. In addition, the bill provided for the distribution of forty-acre allotments of land to the freedmen from the public lands of the states.

Second, a Civil Rights Act, intended to be permanent in its application. It based citizenship on birth in the United States, regardless of race or color, and provided for all citizens the equal protection of the law "as is enjoyed by white citizens." Federal courts were to have jurisdiction in cases arising under it.

Both of these measures were introduced by Senator Trumbull. They were necessary, he thought, in view of the breakdown of law and order in the South and of passage of the Black Codes; he believed they did not necessarily involve Negro suffrage. He further believed that he had Johnson's tacit approval. Congress passed both measures with overwhelming majorities.

Third, an amendment to the Constitution spelling out a new basis for representation in the House of Representatives. To avoid the problem of the South claiming expanded representation on the basis of all its Negro population (even though freedmen could not vote) the joint committee proposed that states disfranchising citizens should lose a proportional number of representatives. In this case, another leading Senator thought he had Johnson's cooperation. Fessenden discussed the proposed amendment at length with the President and went away persuaded that Johnson would support it.

The hopes of Trumbull and Fessenden proved illusory. In vetoes of the Freedmen's Bureau and Civil Rights measures Johnson flatly challenged Congress' authority to act. The Southern states, he wrote, had already "been fully restored," were entitled to exercise their "constitutional rights as members of the Union," and until those rights were recognized Congress had no authority to legislate on Southern affairs. In the meantime, the President, as the sole representative of the entire people in the American structure of government, was duty bound to assert the "just claims" of the excluded Southern states. In short, the President, rather than Congress, possessed the power to direct Reconstruction.

Johnson also addressed himself to the racial aspects of the bills. The

Freedmen's Bureau extension was both unjustified and unnecessary, he wrote: unjustified because protection of freedmen's rights rested with the states; unnecessary because the states, in order to keep their labor, would treat the Negroes fairly. The Civil Rights bill was discriminatory, "in favor of the colored and against the white race." Its conferring of citizenship by virtue of birth in the United States was unfair to foreigners who had to wait five years for citizenship; Negroes, equally unfamiliar with American laws and institutions, should also be subject to a probationary period. Indeed, the measure sought to bring about racial equality and to use federal authority for that end, although it had often been held "expedient to discriminate between the two races."

The vetoes chilled the possibility of further moderate cooperation with the President. Trumbull and Fessenden, feeling themselves victims of bad faith, led the Republican fight to repass the measures. Frustrated by lack of the necessary two-thirds vote in their effort to save the Freedmen's Bureau bill, the Republicans threw scruples to the winds to override the veto of the Civil Rights Act. Their success, as Eric McKitrick has pointed out, marked the first time in American history that a presidential veto of an important piece of legislation had been overridden.[6] It also indicated Republican determination to have Congress establish its own Reconstruction policy.

The basic lines of this policy were set forth in the proposed Fourteenth Amendment, the product of months of debate and so much compromising between radicals, moderates, and conservatives that it aroused little enthusiasm among any of them. Its great virtue was that it provided a "safe" political solution to an explosive problem. There was no hint of confiscation, no mention of direct Negro suffrage. Denial of the right to vote to citizens was to result in a proportionate decrease in a state's representation in Congress. Confederate leaders were barred from holding office, but Congress, by a two-thirds vote, could remove the disability. The national debt of the United States was guaranteed; the debts of the Confederacy, including those of the states, and claims for emancipation of slaves, were outlawed. Leading Johnson newspapers endorsed the measure as not only moderate but in line with the President's thinking.

But Johnson would have none of it. Congress, he repeated, should not pass on Southern questions while Southern representatives were barred. Giving substance to his words, he counselled Southern states to refuse ratification. They complied. The amendment was stalled—and

⁶ McKitrick, *op. cit.*, p. 323.

Republican orators and editors in the North had still another argument to prove their contention that the South was trying to overturn the verdict of the war.

Johnson was not content to block adoption of the Fourteenth Amendment. He passed over to the political offensive in an attempt to purge his administration of Republican opposition. He dismissed from federal service followers of his opponents (who now included moderates and conservatives) and called for the defeat of anti-Johnson Republicans in the fall elections of 1866. To assure such defeat he committed the prestige of his office to active intervention in the campaign, embarking on a speaking tour of Northern cities to persuade the voters to his cause.

The result was disastrous. His maudlin and intemperate speeches, made to order for the ridicule of humorist Petroleum V. Nasby, alienated the still uncommitted. They contributed substantially to the eventual break with the President of such loyal followers as Henry Ward Beecher, the New York *Times,* and the New York *Herald.* When the votes were counted, Republicans had won more than a two-thirds control of Congress.

The Johnson program had failed. The moderate Republican plan had foundered in the face of presidential opposition. Now conditions were propitious for yet another experiment in Reconstruction—Congressional Reconstruction.

Congressional Reconstruction, while it arose out of these problems and conflicts, was conditioned immediately by a complicated political struggle involving the various Republican groups, Northern Democrats, and the President. Much of the significance of this struggle, except as it represented a continuation of past politics, derived from events taking place after the elections of 1866 and during the period early in 1867 when Reconstruction legislation was being considered.

In December, 1866, the Supreme Court, reversing its own position in the Vallandigham case of 1864, handed down its formal opinion in *ex parte Milligan,* declaring unlawful the functioning of military commissions in areas where the civil courts were open. Although the decision grew out of a Civil War case, the court, by implication, denied the legality of the military courts operating in the South under the Supplementary Freedmen's Bureau act passed over presidential veto in July, 1866. Thus, the only protection afforded freedmen and Southern and Northern Unionists against the bias of Southern courts, was endangered. The decision, said Thaddeus Stevens, was "perhaps not as infamous as the Dred Scott decision," but it was "far more dangerous in its operation upon the lives and liberties of the loyal men of this country. That decision has taken away every protection in every one of these rebel States from every loyal man, black or white, who resides there."

Fears of Republicans more moderate than Stevens were stimulated by Johnson's response to the ruling. He ordered dismissal of all trials of civilians by military courts in the South, including those of men accused of murder of Union soldiers and Negroes. He also intervened directly in two notorious cases, one involving South Carolinians found guilty of murder of federal soldiers and the other a Virginia doctor who blandly confessed murder of a Negro for a trivial offense. In both instances the accused went free. Republicans were further aroused by the President's removal of some army commanders in the South and their replacement with appointees more acceptable to white Southerners, by his issuance of secret orders to commanders without informing either Secretary of War Edwin Stanton or General of the Army Grant, and by his overruling orders of commanders to which whites had objected.

The white South, following the lead of the President and of Northern Democrats, continued its policy of non-cooperation. Persecution of Negroes and white Unionists went on unabated; the courts routinely freed white men accused of crimes in such activity. Federal commanders told Congress it was impossible to obtain justice in the courts for either Negroes or white Union men. Responding to the President, legislature after legislature rejected the Fourteenth Amendment. Newspapers counselled their readers to hold firm against any concessions to Northern opinion. Even at the height of Congressional debate on Reconstruction legislation the Memphis *Appeal* said that Negro suffrage was such a "curse and inconceivable calamity" that if enacted it would justify "annihilation" of the Negro race.

In this, the white South was following suggestions of the Northern Democratic press. According to such newspapers, reconstruction legislation was the work of a fanatical Radical minority; the Fourteenth Amendment was a fraud, the acceptance of which would be dishonorable to the South; and in any case the South had nothing to fear. A state could not be lawfully coerced into adopting a constitutional amendment. If Congress passed new laws directed against the South, they would be struck down by the Supreme Court. In addition, the South had the powerful support of the President and the Democratic party. If the South stood firm, moderate opinion in the North would turn against the Radicals and their Reconstruction schemes would fail. Most Southern editors agreed that this was "good advice."

Such advice was part of the larger strategy of Congressional Democrats to bring about a stalemate in Congress and thus thwart Republican plans for Reconstruction. Since their weakness made it impossible for Democrats to block such plans if Republicans were united, the former sought to prevent any rapprochement between moderate Republicans and the President on the one hand, and on the other strove to take advantage of Republican divisions by giving support now to Radicals and then to moderates as circumstances seemed to dictate during the prolonged and bitter debates and confused parliamentary maneuvering which marked consideration of the Reconstruction measure introduced by Stevens at the opening of Congress.

Differences between Radicals and moderates were deep enough and bitter enough to give plausibility to the Democratic program. Radicals, led by Stevens, wanted to impose military government indefinitely on the South, bar Confederate officials from public life for at least five years, and readmit states only when they had accepted Negro suffrage and otherwise complied with Congressional wishes—although even then there was no guarantee of readmission. Moderates, while agreeable to temporary military rule, proposed that clear terms for readmission be set forth, such as acceptance of Negro suffrage and ratification of the Fourteenth Amendment; that the South be left free to comply with such terms on its own initiative; and that when compliance was accomplished, the states should be fully restored.

Given this dissension in Republican ranks, the Democratic plan worked—up to a point. No doubt Democratic counsels helped reinforce Johnson's belief in the rightness of his course, but he had no intention of compromising with Republicans, in any case. In Congress, Democratic maneuvering, coupled with Republican factionalism, did help delay passage of legislation until the closing days of the session—at which point the imperative need for Republican unity to produce some kind of legislation resulted in a bill so vague on the one hand, so full of compromises on the other, that it proved unworkable. The Democrats, by their strategy, had not only failed to block Reconstruction legislation, they had also assured, through their aid to Radicals in voting down moderate proposals, that in part at least Reconstruction would be Radical.

The law which thus emerged declared that since no legal governments existed in Southern states (outside of Tennessee) it was necessary to subject them to the military authority of the United States. To that end, the South was divided into five military districts, each subject to control by a general officer, who was given sweeping powers to maintain "peace and good order"; any interference with him "under color of State authority" was held "null and void." Military authorities could use local courts to punish offenders (despite the act's declaration that no legal governments existed) or could establish military tribunals for that purpose. Thus Congress ignored the spirit, if not the letter, of *ex parte Milligan.*

Restoration of the states to membership in the Union was provided for according to the following formula:

1. Each state constitution must be amended to make it conform to the Constitution of the United States "in all respects."
2. The amendments must be made by a convention elected on the basis of universal male suffrage, including Negroes but barring felons and those "excluded from . . . holding office" under terms of the Fourteenth Amendment. No such excluded person could serve as a member of a convention.
3. The state constitutions must be amended to provide for universal male suffrage.
4. The new constitution must be approved by a majority of voters under such qualifications as applied to convention elections.
5. The new constitution must be approved by Congress.
6. The legislature elected under the new constitution must ratify the Fourteenth Amendment.
7. The state would be re-admitted when these requirements had been met and *the Fourteenth Amendment had become part of the Constitution of the United States.* Thus, no individual state could attain full membership in the Union until other states had accepted the Fourteenth Amendment.

Until re-admission, existing state governments were held to be "provisional," subject to the "paramount authority" of the United States.

Johnson, in a carefully reasoned veto challenging the constitutionality of the measure, also raised the race issue. The bill, he said, forced "the right of suffrage out of the hands of the white people and into the hands of the negroes." These, he said, "have not asked for the privilege of voting; the vast majority of them have no idea what it means." Indeed, he insinuated, the bill represented a policy of "Africanizing the southern part of our territory." The veto was overridden.

The President, of course, was far off the mark in attributing such a design to his opponents; he was equally mistaken in asserting that Negroes did not want the franchise.

Frederick Douglass spoke for his people when he said, "Slavery is not abolished until the black man has the ballot." The *Cincinnati*

Colored Citizen noted that the "whole difficulty, . . . , of [presidential] reconstruction springs from an unwillingness to carry out democratic principles." The National Equal Rights League petitioned Congress to invalidate all state laws discriminating against Negroes.

Negro conventions in South Carolina, North Carolina, Tennessee, Virginia, and Mississippi all called for voting rights. A meeting of Negroes in Petersburg, Virginia, recalled the Civil War record of Negro troops, pointed out the services of Negroes in the Revolutionary War and the War of 1812, and in words reminiscent of those of 1776, declared, "representation and taxation go hand in hand, and it is diametrically opposed to Republican institutions, to tax us for the support and expense of the Government, and deny us at the same time, the right of representation."

The Reconstruction law of March 2, 1867, met that argument, in principle, by requiring Negro suffrage. But it provided no way for putting the principle into effect, apart from leaving it to Southern whites to take the initiative in complying with the law's conditions for readmission. Naturally, Southerners saw little advantage in such a course when they could continue to live under Johnson governments, even if they were "provisional" and subject to military control. Johnson, as commander-in-chief, could be depended upon to make that control tolerable—an expectation which turned out to be fully justified. In addition, Southern states could, and did, move in the courts to enjoin enforcement of the law. That the attempts failed is of less significance than that the filing of the suits indicated that the white South had little intention of compliance. But if worse came to worst, Southerners could always frustrate adoption of new constitutions by refraining from voting, as did Alabamians, taking advantage of the law's stipulation that approval of such constitutions required a majority of all registered voters, not simply a majority of those actually voting.

Confronted with Southern resistance, Johnson's evident determination to enforce the law as he interpreted it, and its own failure to spell out the steps for implementation, Congress responded with three additional acts (March 23 and July 19, 1867, and March 11, 1868). These, in summary, provided for voter registration, tightened up disfranchisement provisions, conferred on military commanders authority to organize elections of constitutional conventions, and allowed new constitutions to be adopted by a majority of votes cast. To further assure its control over Reconstruction, Congress also passed legislation curtailing the power of the President to remove appointive officials and restricting his authority as commander-in-chief. It also withdrew recently granted authority to the Supreme Court to hear appeals on writs of *habeas corpus,* an action which effectively closed the door of the court to Southern whites who fell afoul of the military tribunals.

This, then, was the general framework of Southern Reconstruction. How did the Black South—and the white—fare under it?

CHAPTER 2

Type-Casting the Negro

The importance of the political settlement cannot be underestimated. It assured Republican hegemony sufficient time during this crucial period to imbed in national policy the ambivalent lavishing of governmental benevolence on business on the one hand while maintaining a *laissez-faire* hostility to social reform on the other. It helped make possible the penetration of the South by Northern industry and finance. It fashioned the political institutions through which white and black Southerners attempted to meet their specific problems. And, by no means least, by its failure to provide land for the impoverished freedman it type-cast him in the role of propertyless laborer. This, combined with the racial attitudes of whites in both North and South, effectively circumscribed the part which the Negro could play in fashioning his destiny from that day to ours.

This danger was foreseen by friends of the freedmen, and found specific expression in the repeated attempts of Thaddeus Stevens to secure confiscation of large Confederate estates and distribute a portion of the 394 million acres so obtained among the Negroes. "If we do not furnish them with homesteads and hedge them around with protective laws; . . . we had better have left them in bondage," he told Congress in 1865. He proposed that each adult male freedman be given 40 acres, which, in his estimate, would total about 40 million acres. The remainder of the confiscated land would be divided into farms and sold to the highest bidders. The income was to be used to help retire the national debt, increase the pensions of Union war veterans, and provide compensation for Unionists who suffered property losses during the war.

Even this skillfully contrived program, offering even more to whites than it did to Negroes, could make no headway, then or later. It was too repugnant to the prevailing belief, almost religious in its intensity, that in a free society like America's there were no limits to an individual's attainments if he were industrious, frugal, and ambitious and free from governmental interference. Now that the Negro was free, he too could share in the manifold opportunities unfolding in an expanding country; he was in no more need of special governmental protection than the white man.

This view was shared by men otherwise so opposed as William Lloyd Garrison and Andrew Johnson. Garrison argued that with abolition, racial prejudice, "the natural product of the [slavery] system," would eventually disappear and Negroes would "win their way to wealth, distinction, eminence, and official station." Johnson, in vetoing the Freedmen's Bureau bill in 1866, expressed the hope that instead of relying on governmental protection the Negroes would, "by their own efforts, establish for themselves a condition of responsibility and prosperity. It is certain that they can attain that condition only through their own merits and exertions." Indeed, he said, "The idea upon which slaves were assisted to freedom was that they become a self-sustaining population."

The proposal of confiscation also offended the traditional American respect for private property. Even during the war Lincoln had threatened to veto the second Confiscation Act unless it were drastically modified —and Congress yielded. Even so, the Administration made little effort to enforce the law. Now, with the war over, *The Nation* denounced "the assumption that the distribution of other people's land to the Negroes is necessary to complete the work of emancipation," saying that "division of rich men's lands among the landless . . . would give a shock to our whole social and political system from which it could hardly recover without the loss of liberty." More bluntly, Rep. John W. Chanler of New York, called confiscation "robbery . . . the tool of the tyrant and the oppressor." Friends of Stevens urged him to abandon his crusade lest it endanger the Republican majority in Congress.

Apart from considerations of principle and ideology, there were interests opposed to land distribution. Some Northern businessmen saw in poor Negroes a handy instrument with which to fight the rising power of labor unions. Others, with an eye to investment in Southern plantations, railroads, and industries, felt it advisable to maintain a large pool of Negro labor on which to draw when the need arose. Southern planters, and most Southern whites, naturally wanted to keep the Negro in a dependent state. All of these elements—not least the white South—had spokesmen and allies in Congress and the White House.

Thus it came about that the Reconstruction program was narrowly political, paying little heed to the economic adjustments necessary if emancipation were to be meaningful. With the exception of minor distribution of public lands, which will be discussed later, Congress failed to follow up its promising precedent in the original Freedmen's Bureau bill. This, as Frederick Douglass pointed out, made the program "radically defective." The Russian serfs, he noted, had been granted land when they were freed in 1861; in contrast, American slaves "were sent away empty-handed, without money, . . . without a foot of land upon which to stand. Old and young, sick and well, were turned loose to the open sky, naked to their enemies."

White Southerners, of course, denied they were "enemies." Their view was succinctly stated by N. B. Forrest, the Ku Klux Klan leader and former Confederate general: "I am not an enemy of the Negro. We want him here among us; he is the only laboring class we have." That is, the white South was prepared to accept the Negro—not as citizen, not as independent farmer, not as a man, but as menial laborer, looking to the whites for sustenance. Ironically, the Reconstruction measures, so hated by most white Southerners, enabled them to have their way.

When it became apparent that the Federal Government was not going to underwrite the economic independence of the freedmen, they perforce had to accommodate themselves to the harsh realities of a "free" labor market in which they had little bargaining power. This accommodation in turn was shaped by larger influences which determined the course of Southern economic development for generations to come.

These grew out of the basic reality of the South as an extractive, colonial economy. It was extractive in the sense that it produced raw materials, principally cotton, which were manufactured elsewhere; colonial, in that to carry on its work, it had to depend on "foreign" capital. Therefore the South was economically tributary, both in the prices it received for its products and the prices it had to pay to produce them.

This had been true of the pre-war South, of course, but its plight was now accentuated by the destruction of so much capital during the war and by its having to compete for capital in a post-war economy in which capital was in relatively short supply. The national boom in railroading and manufacturing called for investment on such a scale that American investors could not cope with it. The lucrative prospects thus revealed encouraged foreign capitalists to increase their American holdings, which by 1869 amounted to $1,390,000,000—and thereafter increased steadily. The result was that interest rates were high, even on "gilt edge" securities—and much higher on speculative ventures such as cotton growing. In such a situation those in the South who had capital—and these included Northerners as well as those Southerners who had somehow contrived to make money out of the war—were in a unique position to command those, white and black, who lacked it.

For planters to operate profitably within this context would have been difficult enough, but there were still other factors which compounded their difficulties. The pre-war domination of the world market by Southern cotton was gone; now it had to compete with cotton from India, Latin America, and the Near East—a competition made no easier by the imposition in 1867 of a federal tax of three per cent, applicable to exports as well as to domestic consumption. Never during Reconstruction did cotton exports approach the 1860 total of 1,768,-000,000 pounds; by 1876 they finally did reach 1,491,000,000 pounds—but in six of the ten post-war years they fell below a billion pounds each. The value of the exports, although fluctuating from year to year, showed a strong tendency to decline: in 1866 sales abroad were valued at 281 million dollars; in 1876, at 193 million dollars.

In addition, while the planter was selling on a free, competitive world market, he was buying on a domestic market protected by tariffs and increasingly controlled at the price level by emerging trusts and other instruments of consolidation. In short, the planter was in the unenviable—almost impossible—business situation of having to sell cheap and buy dear.

He was also confronted with the fact that the more he produced, the less he got—especially after the collapse of the national economy which began in 1873 and outlasted Reconstruction. By 1876 the pre-war cotton production record was surpassed: 4,474,000 bales in that year as compared to 3,841,000 bales in 1860—a suggestive commentary on the industry of black labor, dominant in the cotton economy. Prices set a record in the other direction. In 1869, the first year for which comparable figures can be obtained, cotton sold at 16.5 cents a pound; in 1876 it sold at 9.7 cents, a decline of 41 per cent. The same held true for tobacco. Production rose from 316,495,000 pounds in 1866 to 466,050,000 ten years later; in the same period prices fell 37 per cent, from 11.6 to 7.3 cents a pound. Figures for sugar production do not seem available, but price statistics show a fall of 38.5 per cent between 1866 and 1876.

Unfortunately, there are no reliable statistics on prices the planter had to pay for goods he required: equipment, fertilizer, seed, food, and clothing not only for his own family but often also for those of his laborers. Two sets of figures give a rough indication of national trends:

in the period, 1866–1876, wholesale commodity prices (including that of cotton) dropped 37 per cent, while living costs declined only 21 per cent. This in itself might warrant an inference that prices the planter received declined more sharply than his costs; but there was another element, unique to Southern agriculture, which pressed the planter even more. This was his indebtedness to the country merchant (whom we shall discuss shortly) for operating capital; and the merchant inflated both his prices and his interest charges. Thus, even if the planter were not at a disadvantage in terms of national trends, he was very much so in terms of his own immediate situation: in an era of falling prices he was compelled to pay off debts, at high interest, contracted when prices were higher on the goods he sold.

One solution suggested itself—a solution similar to that adopted by Northern manufacturers in economic difficulties: cut costs. In particular, this meant labor costs. In the South this was perhaps easier than in the North: unions among farm laborers were unheard of, the laborers were so poor they had no resources to resist, and the mass of them were black men, doubly vulnerable because of their race and their identification with the Yankee conqueror. Planters took full advantage of the Negro plight: wages were reduced, allowances cut to bare subsistence, housing to a wretched minimum. This availed the planters little. While the Negro in general sank into peonage, they themselves were so caught in the web of debt that some gave up, and many others sank into tenantry, often on the very lands they once owned. Like the black man, the white planter was bound to a cash-crop economy which fastened poverty on the rural South.

This development came about gradually during Reconstruction as whites and blacks sought pragmatically to solve their economic problems within the new framework of free labor. Early attempts to adjust to a money-wage system broke down. Some planters simply lacked the cash to meet regular payrolls; others believed such a system would not work with Negroes; still others were opposed on principle—wages would make the Negro too independent. Negroes, on the other hand, preferred money wages, and where possible, refused to work on any other basis. Often, though, they found they had contributed unpaid labor: some planters could not pay, and others swindled the Negroes out of their wages. On the other hand, Negroes, unaccustomed to the discipline of a wage system, resented supervision as an infringement on their freedom, and when paid, took time off to enjoy the new-found pleasure of spending their own money. Planters complained that this demonstrated Negro "irresponsibility." Bosses in Western logging camps and on railroad construction jobs could have told them that white workers behaved much the same way on pay day.

Some planters, as in Louisiana, organized to put payment of wages on an annual basis; Negroes would be granted "a small advance for clothing, medicine, etc.," which, said the planters, was "all that can reasonably be demanded, or safely made." They further recommended that wages, instead of being set by the supply and demand of the labor market, be determined by the price of cotton. As a Negro newspaper pointed out, this meant that if "cotton be depreciated on the market the laborer will have to starve, while the planter will keep the little money he may make by selling it."

Others thought to solve the problem by importing foreign laborers in great numbers. In Mississippi, for example, it was commonly believed that docile Chinese coolies could be obtained who would work for four dollars a month and feed and clothe themselves; various schemes were set on foot to bring these nonpareils of cheap labor into the state. Other states, as well as Mississippi, tried to stimulate European immigration through new state agencies or private companies.

Such projects proved impractical. Chinese coolies could not be had for less than twelve dollars a month, plus transportation and rations more substantial than those provided Negroes; in addition, they were unfamiliar with the techniques of cotton agriculture. The few Europeans who came found conditions and wages intolerable, jumped their contracts, and headed for more congenial society elsewhere. White employers had to accept the fact that while the free Negro was unwelcome they could not survive without him. Their point of view was expressed by a writer in the Louisville *Journal*, who concluded, after employing Northerners, Swedes, Canadians, Dutch, and Irish, "I prefer the Negro to any of them. The Negro is not so quick as many white laborers, but he demands so much less in the way of supplies, is more acclimated, and generally easier to get along with."

If white employers came to realize that they needed the Negro, it was no less true that the landless, propertyless Negro perceived he depended on white employers. Out of this mutual need and the breakdown of the money-wage system came a pragmatic solution—sharecropping, an arrangement whereby the planter rented out a parcel of land to the Negro in return for a share of the crop. Practice varied from place to place, but in general the Negro received a third, the planter another third, and the remainder went to the merchant who provided food, clothing, and necessary supplies.

It was at this last point that the evils of the system became manifest.

The South, as we have seen, was short of capital and credit. Cotton growing, like all agricultural enterprise, was heavily dependent on credit over the growing season. Someone had to furnish the means for food, clothing, fertilizer, and equipment until the crop was marketed; and someone had to furnish the contacts necessary for selling the crop. Since the pre-war cotton factor, or broker, was largely gone, the vacuum was filled by Northerners and by native white "new men" as thoroughly imbued with the business point of view as the Yankee.

Setting themselves up in towns and villages, these country merchants provided the necessary credit for the supplies they sold at mark-ups ranging from 20 to 200 per cent—and the cost of the credit came high. To insure their loans the merchants took liens (mortgages) on the crop and mortgages on land and chattels. Since the merchants, in turn, depended on credit from other sources, on which they had to pay interest of 12 to 36 per cent, they insisted on borrowers planting only readily marketable cash crops, such as cotton and tobacco.

Caught in a debt squeeze, trapped in a cash crop economy, the independent planter had still another burden to bear: higher taxes. Before the war, taxes, especially on land, had been phenomenally low; the burden of taxation lay rather on business and the professions, although planters paid some taxation on their slaves. That was all changed. Slave property was gone. Business interests were successful in having Reconstruction governments shift the burden of taxation to land. This would have meant a higher tax bill for planters in any case— but in addition the costs of government had gone up.

Costs were higher because state and local governments had to repair the ravages of war: bridges and roads had to be rebuilt, public buildings restored. Also, the Reconstruction governments undertook new, ambitious, and expensive social programs, such as free public school systems; care for the poor, aged, and infirm; building of asylums for the mentally ill and prisons for criminals. Thus, taxes were bound to go up, even if all the state and local governments had been run by honest men. But this was an era when honesty in public affairs was rare—not only in the South but throughout the nation, including the national government. Thus, the legitimate work of government plus corruption forced tax rates up. They never went as high as those of Northern states, but this was little consolation to planters accustomed to a tax structure which had favored them and who now were overwhelmed by debt.

In a period of falling prices it became increasingly difficult for planters to pay both higher taxes and their debts. Some became delinquent in their taxes; their lands were sold at public auction to the affluent. If some Republicans believed in higher taxes as a matter of

public policy, in that it would lead to the sale of small plots to
Negro farmers, their plans miscarried. Few Negroes possessed either the
cash or credit to take advantage of the land sales; most of the land
passed to whites, Northern and Southern, who did have cash and
credit.

Many other planters, who could meet their taxes, could not meet their
debts—and their lands passed into the hands of the merchants who
foreclosed their mortgages. Those planters who did not turn to other
vocations became tenants: the exact number of dispossessed is difficult
to fix, but there is little doubt it was substantial. This destruction of an
independent Southern yeomanry had profound psychological consequences for Reconstruction—consequences all too little studied.

Recent studies by sociologists and psychologists indicate that people
in process of losing status ("downward social mobility") display more
ethnic hostility than more stable groups; and this hostility, carried
to the point of violence, becomes more intense during periods of
economic distress. Both of these elements were present in marked
degree during Reconstruction. As the formerly independent white
planter found himself driven down the social scale closer to the Negro,
his attitudes became those of the traditional poor white. To the new
poor white, as to the old, the assertion of white supremacy became
a psychological necessity.

It was also a safe, and eventually effective, way of venting his
frustration at the new order of things. The Federal Government, the
credit system, the traditional Establishment of property—all these
were beyond his reach, invulnerable. But white Republicans and Negroes were within reach—and vulnerable. Against the black men, the
feeling of the displaced white planter was most bitter, for they sat in
the legislatures which voted the high taxes, and participated, even if
on a minor scale, in the corruption. In the mind of the impoverished
planter, it was they, literally black Republicans, who were in great
part responsible for his plight.

Such a situation was intolerable—to the white, it was the rule of
poverty over property, ignorance over intelligence. From finding the
situation intolerable it was but a step to justifying any means to end
it, even if that meant violence. And violence there was, sometimes
restrained, sometimes not. The black man must be kept "in his place."

The Negro, economically speaking, was already "in his place." If
the white planter was a victim of the crop lien system, the black laborer
was doubly so, for he was both poor and black. Usually lacking even

the rudiments of education, he had to accept work on the planter's terms, take the planter's word for the value of his crop, and accept the merchant's decision as to his debt. Many croppers found that at the end of the year their crop was insufficient to pay off their debts; to get new loans they had to pledge the next year's crop and pay higher interest rates. Faced with ever mounting debt, some simply left their plots of land and wandered elsewhere in search of better conditions; others simply sank into peonage, virtual slaves of the merchants, who, as has been noted, increasingly took over the lands of the planters.

Planters, desperately trying to save their lands, had strong incentive to wring every penny out of the croppers; merchants, plagued with bad debts but eager to add to their small capital, felt few scruples about taking advantage of either white planter or illiterate Negro. As Edward King observed after long travels through the South in 1873 and 1874: "He [the Negro] has entered upon a battle-field armed with poor and cumbersome weapons, weighed down with ignorance and 'previous condition'; no one feels the difficulty and bitterness of his position more keenly than he does himself."

The Negro knew only too well how difficult his position was. Planters threatened him with eviction if he dabbled in Republican politics. They cut costs by reducing his food and clothing in quality and quantity and by providing only ramshackle housing. In Mississippi they would not rent land to black men. In some areas they set terms among themselves on the wages and allowances of laborers. Some of the more unscrupulous even robbed the Negro of his due by forcibly driving him off the land when the crop was ready. Three such victims told a Congressional committee in 1875 that when they refused to "give up our crop for nothing" one of them was flogged, and "then we got afraid and we left the place." Their bitter comment could have been echoed by many others: "We worked for them [the planters] as though we were slaves, and then [were] treated like dogs all the time."

To threaten legal action was to invite a visit from the Ku Klux Klan. In the unlikely event of getting the matter into court, the Negro stood little chance of a fair hearing, despite all the alleged pro-Negro bias of the Reconstruction governments. As a convention of Alabama Negroes pointed out in a memorial to Congress in 1874, juries in such cases were always made up of white men, and, "In controversies between our race and white men, . . . , it is almost if not quite impossible for a black man to obtain justice." In South Carolina, however, the local magistrates' courts, which passed on small claims, seem to have accorded some degree of justice—or so one may judge from the comments of disgruntled planters who felt the courts should have accepted *their* claims in whole.

Negroes sought to escape the evils of sharecropping in two ways: renting land, or owning it. Renting would give them more freedom than sharecropping in managing their affairs; in good years it furnished the prospect of improved income. If crops were poor, the renter could always move! In addition, renting meant improved status—the Negro could be much more independent as renter than as cropper.

This, of course, clashed with the white determination to keep the black man in a subordinate position. It also ran counter to what the planter conceived to be his economic interest. He wanted full control of his labor, and he wanted his full proportionate share of the crop, in good and bad years alike. In South Carolina it was argued also that black men could not be depended upon to maintain rented property. Some Mississippi citizens argued more bluntly that any white man who rented to Negroes was a public enemy.

The result was that the number of black renters always remained small throughout the South.

The other alternative was land ownership. Negroes who could find the means tried to acquire land. When Congress, in June 1866, threw open for homesteading public lands in Southern states, Negroes eagerly responded, although Congress appropriated no funds for resettlement. They took up 160,960 acres in Florida and occupied 116 of 243 available homesteads in Arkansas. Altogether more than 4,000 families took up land. Unfortunately, much of the land was poor, the Negroes encountered white hostility, and—as usual in such disposition of public lands—most of the good land fell into the hands of white speculators.

Since, apart from this minor program, Congress did nothing to assure land for the freedmen, they turned to the states. Except for South Carolina the Reconstruction governments were indifferent. In that state an expensive land distribution project—expensive largely because so much corruption was involved—eventually resulted in nearly 2,000 families getting homesteads. Theoretically, Negroes might have benefitted from tax sales by both federal and state governments— that is, sale of land for tax delinquency. In practice, because they had insufficient cash and credit was hard to get, Negroes gained little from such expropriation. Well-to-do native whites and Yankees gained a great deal.

Negroes, then, were forced back on whatever resources they had. In many localities they pooled their funds in cooperative associations, bought lands and worked them in accord with agreements reached among themselves. Two such groups developed prosperous plantations in the South Carolina Sea Islands. In Virginia, Negroes formed building and loan associations to help finance farm purchases: by the early 70's Negroes owned between 80,000 and 100,000 acres in the state. In Georgia, black farmers owned 339,000 acres by 1874. Everywhere, black men and women saved and scrimped to gather together enough cash to get land they could call their own. In some areas, however, even cash could not get them land. In some sections of Mississippi, for example, whites simply would not sell to Negroes.

The Negro desire for land, combined with their ignorance and helplessness, opened the way for unscrupulous whites. Some Negroes were "sold" land lacking valid titles. Others purchased land which turned out to be "so poor they could not raise a peck of corn to the acre." Men who held valid legal title to land in the South Carolina Sea Islands lost it for alleged nonpayment of a land tax. In areas where white hostility ran high, Negro landholders were driven out by violence. A resident of Clay County, Florida, told a Congressional committee in 1871 that when she and her husband refused to give up land for which they had paid $150 they were brutally flogged by Klansmen and their property destroyed.

Other factors worked against permanent Negro land ownership. Freedmen might know how to cultivate cotton and tobacco, but most had no skill in farm management and little knowledge of financing. They possessed little capital, and white merchants and banks were reluctant to lend to independent black proprietors. One or two bad years—adverse weather, insect pests, plant diseases, poor crops—were usually sufficient to end the ownership of the black yeoman.

Dispossessed white yeomen, as we have seen, could vent their frustrations safely in aggression against Negroes and white Republicans. Dispossessed black yeomen had no such outlet. Confronted with the overwhelming power of a hostile society, they turned their frustrations against themselves. Since, despite their best efforts, they were going nowhere, why bother? This feeling of futility, embracing both former landowners and those who never owned land, helps explain, in part, the loss of initiative which beset so many Negroes in the 70's and later.

Although the proportion of black men who were able to buy and to keep land was small, it is significant. It is an indication that in the face of great difficulties, some Negroes were able to cope successfully with the problems of living in a society in which the race was to the swift and the battle to the strong. By their very being they helped disprove the claim that black men could not survive in a competitive society.

As the Negro in the countryside generally lost his struggle to rise up from poverty, so did the skilled worker in the towns and cities wage, and lose, his own battle for economic independence. In his case, the campaign centered around the right to practice his skill as craftsman —as carpenter, shoemaker, blacksmith, engraver, or printer. There were considerable numbers of such men in the North and in the Border States; in 1865 they were said to outnumber white mechanics in the South five to one. In all areas, however, the black craftsman faced implacable opposition: unions barred him, and when employers hired him, white workers walked out. Here was a situation as threatening to Negro independence as was denial of land to the rural laborer. As Isaac Myers, an articulate Baltimore ship caulker, put it, "American citizenship for the black man is a complete failure if he is proscribed from the workshops of the country."

Part of the misfortune of the Negro craftsman lay in the fact that he appeared in large numbers on the free labor market at an unpropitious time. Demobilization of the armies, renewed large-scale immigration, and the post-war depression which began late in 1865 and lasted well into 1867, intensified job competition and heightened rivalries between native whites, immigrants, and Negroes. During the war, skilled white labor, fearful of the loss of status and wages involved in rapid mechanization of industry, spurred on by an inflation which reduced real wages by a third, and encouraged by the demand for labor, organized 13 national unions of craftsmen, covering various workers such as coal miners, iron puddlers, locomotive engineers, bricklayers, and ship carpenters and caulkers. In the post-war period these emerging unions found themselves under attack.

Employers, organized on local, state, and national levels to combat the new unions, broke strikes with the use of strikebreakers, often Negroes, and worked to break unions by lockouts, blacklisting of active union men, and "yellow dog" contracts, which required as a condition of employment that a worker abjure union membership. They were aided by laws directed against union activity, passed during the war by such states as Minnesota, Illinois, and Pennsylvania, and by renewed invocation in the courts of the English common law doctrine of conspiracy, which held it to be a crime against the public interest for laborers to engage in concerted activity to raise wages or otherwise improve conditions of employment.

Into this arena of class conflict was catapulted the Negro craftsman. Barred by the unions, he was easy prey for employers to use for anti-union ends. Now union men hated the Negro not only because of his color, but also because he was the union man's most reprehensible enemy: the "scab." Unions struck back by enforcing the barriers against Negroes; union men walked out when Negro craftsmen appeared on a job. While this made it easier for employers to recruit Negroes as strikebreakers, it also made it increasingly difficult for Negroes to find work at the level of their skills: the engraver who had to make a living as a waiter was all too typical.

The dangers inherent in this situation were clear to thoughtful union men of both races. William H. Sylvis, the pioneer builder of the iron molders' union, strove in 1866 to meet the employers' offensive by promoting a National Labor Union embracing all organized labor; and Isaac Myers, the leading spirit among the Baltimore ship caulkers, sought an organization which would transcend racial lines. Their views were expressed by Andrew C. Cameron, editor of the *Workingman's Advocate* of Chicago, one of the newspapers endorsed by the National Labor Union. Unions, said Cameron, should help "inculcate the grand ennobling idea that the interests of labor are one; that there should be no distinction of race or nationality."

Such appeals fell on deaf ears. The newly founded National Labor Union, while willing to accept Negro delegates from Negro unions, was unwilling to risk its prospects with white unions by espousing the cause of integrated unionism. By 1869 the issue could be evaded no longer, for independent Negro organization was growing rapidly and Negro unions in the NLU were pressing for action, with Myers arguing eloquently that freedom without the right to work at one's trade was meaningless. The NLU convention of that year found a compromise between the demands of the Negroes and the obduracy of white unions: it urged black workers to form their own unions and to send delegates to the NLU. In addition, it set up a special committee to promote Negro unionism in Pennsylvania. As W. E. B. DuBois pointed out, this in effect meant setting up segregated unions which would help curb Negro job competition while keeping Negroes out of the white unions, the centers of real power.

The Carpenters and Joiners National Union, however, followed the Sylvis lead, urging organization of both white and black craftsmen and the admission of qualified Negroes to its existing local unions. This was exceptional. More typical was the attitude of the National Typographical Union. In 1869 it upheld its Washington, D.C., branch in denying membership to Lewis Douglass, son of Frederick Douglass, who was employed in the Government Printing Office. When the issue came before the union convention again in 1870 the delegates voted to leave the issue of Negro membership to the local membership, which meant exclusion.

The rationale offered became common among unions for years to come:

> That there are deep-seated prejudices against the colored race no one will deny; and those prejudices are so strong in many local unions that any attempt to disregard or override them will almost inevitably lead to anarchy and disintegration . . . surely no one who has the welfare of the craft at heart will seriously contend that the union of thousands of white printers should be destroyed for the purpose of granting a barren honor of membership to a few Negroes.

Even the NLU committee set up to promote joint action found the outlook so discouraging that it recommended organization of Jim Crow locals.

Confronted with such attitudes, Negro craftsmen strove to improve their lot and preserve their skills by organizing themselves. Strikes in Mobile, Ala., Charleston, S.C., and Savannah, Ga., in 1867 spurred the formation of central bodies to support and coordinate their efforts. Most notable among these was the Maryland state organization, established in July, 1869, with the persevering Myers as leader. Although voting to attend the NLU convention in August, the Maryland delegates hedged their bet by calling for a national Negro labor convention in December in Washington, D.C.—a call which doubtless influenced the NLU to take its first hesitant steps toward support of Negro unionism.

The convention of 156 delegates was made up largely of non-labor elements, such as lawyers, preachers, and politicians, but it did include representatives from craftsmen and mechanics—and it did mark out a road for labor quite different from that of the NLU. It made "no distinction as to nationality, sex, or color" and appealed specifically to Southern whites, Irishmen, Germans, and Chinese to join together to overcome the racial barriers which prevented the united action of labor. Otherwise, the new organization pointed out, all labor would suffer: "Any labor movement based upon . . . discrimination . . . will prove to be of very little value."

While holding the door open for non-Negro collaboration, even to voting affiliation with the NLU, the convention urged Negroes to proceed with formation of their own unions and to promote establishment of workshops to provide employment for skilled Negroes. To carry out this program a permanent National Labor Bureau was established in Washington, D.C. The bureau was also to work for state protective legislation, to campaign for assurance of legal equality for Negroes, and to enlist popular support for its program through its newspaper, *The New National Era.*

In addition to pioneering in the field of integrated unionism, the National Negro Labor Union also broke ground in another direction. White labor organizations, then as now, were primarily concerned with the problems of urban workers; the NNLU expressed deep concern for the problems of rural labor. In a lengthy memorial to Congress, the union pointed out that Negro agricultural laborers in the South earned less than ten dollars a month and that wages were held down by agreements among planters. Lacking land and the resources necessary for strikes, the Negro laborer was defenseless against such conspiracies; his dependency and defenselessness in turn threatened not only his economic well-being but also his political freedom; if the Negro wanted work at all, he had to vote as his employer dictated. Thus, said the union, "The freedom of the ballot is . . . sought to be subdued by the necessity for bread, and with the loyal colored laborer of the South, duty to his country involves danger to himself."

As a remedy, the union urged Congress to appropriate forty acres to each freedman from the public lands in the South, estimated at more than 46 million acres. In states where no public domain existed, it was recommended that the United States buy land for distribution to freedmen on a 40-acre basis and that lapsed railroad land grants in Southern states be turned over for homesteading by Negroes. Congress, rarely reluctant to heed the pleas of railroad promoters for public lands, showed little interest in this proposal for using the public land policy to establish an independent Negro yeomanry in the South. Instead, in 1876, under pressure from Southern white politicians, Congress abandoned the beginnings of such policy as it had embarked on in 1866.

Possibilities of cooperation between the NLU and the NNLU soon foundered on the rock of politics. Indeed, all along political differences as well as racial prejudice had served to keep white and Negro workers apart. In the heyday of Andrew Johnson white labor had loyally supported him: after all, he was one of them, a humble tailor who had not forgotten his origins and knew first hand the hardships of the workingman; as President he had shown his sympathies by initiating the eight-hour day in government offices and cancelling a projected wage reduction in the War Department. Besides, many labor unionists shared Johnson's fear of an "aristocracy of the dollar"—which they identified with the Republican party.

With the passing of Andrew Johnson from the political scene, those in the NLU who advocated independent political action gained strength, and the organization began to attract non-labor reform elements and politicos who saw opportunities in a labor movement oriented in their direction. These elements became so powerful by 1870 that a union delegate complained that the convention of that year was "a strange mixture of mechanics, workingmen, ministers, lawyers, editors, lobby-ists, and others of no particular occupation." There was not much of a mixture by the following year: only two of the 22 delegates represented labor unions. In turning to politics, the NLU had lost the support of unions interested primarily in collective bargaining: in 1868 it counted five powerful national unions as members; in 1871, it had none.

All of this made little sense to Negro unionists. Like other Negroes they were early disenchanted with Johnson, and they saw no solution to their specific problems in following the will-o'-the-wisp of a labor party, with its talk of currency reform, government ownership of rail-roads, and abolition of the national banking system. DuBois may have exaggerated when he said that "in the South, the Republican party was par excellence the party of labor," but there is no doubt that Negroes looked upon it as *their* party. It had been the political instrument of their freedom; it stood between them and the white terror of the South; and it afforded them the ballot. To them, the last was of prime impor-tance now, for they interpreted the franchise not in purely political terms but in larger socio-economic terms: the ballot would open the way for better jobs, wages, working conditions—and for land.

As the Negro labor newspaper, *The New National Era,* put it: the ballot would "lubricate the corroded hinges upon which swing wide open the portals of the temple of industry, closed against the Northern Colored Man's right to labor, and which can only be opened by the talismanic word of two syllables, viz.: the ballot." Negro unionists were not likely to follow white advice to desert their own party—especially when the advice came from unionists who kept the doors of workshops closed against Negroes.

The issue came to a head in the 1870 convention of the NLU, when the organization was already suffering from secession of major unions and invasion of middle-class reformers and politicians. Some unionists joined with the latter groups in proposing a labor party, making an appeal to Negro delegates that "inasmuch as both the present political parties are dominated by the non-producing classes, the highest interest of our colored fellow-citizens is with the workingmen, who, like them-selves, are slaves of capital and politicians."

The Negroes were not impressed. Their spokesman, Isaac Myers, argued that while the Democrats were hostile to all labor, white and black, the Republicans were friendly, and that only through them could necessary labor legislation be obtained. To be sure, the Republican party was "not the beau ideal of our notion of a party," he conceded, but "the interests of workingmen demand that they shall not hazard its success either by the organization of a new party or by an affiliation with the Democratic party." The white majority, unimpressed, went on to call for a third party. This, together with the convention's failure to address itself to the problems of Negro labor, led to withdrawal by the NNLU.

Promotion of long-range political objectives at the expense of short-range union goals helped bring about the demise of the NLU. Such also was the fate of the Negro organization. At its convention in 1870 it endorsed the Republicans, and under the new leadership of Frederick Douglass was converted into a partisan apparatus. Through 1871 some grass roots union activities were continued, including the organization of a longshoremen's union in Baltimore, which marked its debut by winning, without a strike, a wage increase of 25 per cent—from 20 cents to 25 cents an hour. Such actions became increasingly rare as men like Myers faded from the scene and politicians like Douglass came to the fore. Less and less attention was paid to the needs of Negro labor as the union became racked by political dissension, between rival Republican groups and between Republicans and the small but growing number of Negro Democrats.

Thus, when the economic storm of 1873 burst upon the country, neither white nor black labor possessed a comprehensive national organization with which to protect themselves. It is ironic that a year later, while the depression still spiralled downwards, the official publication of the NNLU, edited by Douglass, expounded on "The Folly, Tyranny, and Wickedness of Labor Unions."

The "lily white" policies of the unions, however, had helped set the conditions which frustrated black craftsmen in their search for improved economic and social status. Combined with lack of white patronage for Negro craftsmen, the barring of their entry into new and their confinement to declining industries, and displacement of black by white workers in such well-paying jobs as barbers and hotel waiters, such policies contributed no little to the shrinking of the proportion of skilled Negro workers which was evident by the 90's.

Racial exclusiveness and fear of Negro competition was not confined to the ranks of labor, however. Whites in professional fields reacted to the entrance of Negroes with the same hostility demonstrated by union men. A case in point was that of the Medical Society of the

District of Columbia. After the war a number of Negro physicans, including some who had served with the Union Army, settled in that city and applied for admission to the society, because, as they later pointed out, it was the "only one medical society in the District where all licenses to practice must be obtained, and all advantages flowing from medical and professional discussions were to be enjoyed." Despite the fact that the applicants were passed by the society's Board of Examiners, the society rejected them on grounds of race. In addition, the society replaced the chairman of the examining board with a doctor who had served with the Confederate Army, "well known for his opposition to the admission of colored physicians."

When the Negro physicians petitioned Congress to grant a charter for a new medical organization basing membership on purely professional qualifications, the society denounced them for malicious and false attacks in calling attention to its discriminatory practices!

The Negroes organized their own society, the National Medical Society of the District of Columbia. Similar experiences among teachers, insurance men, lawyers, and bankers led to their forming their own local and eventually national Negro associations.

While Negroes strove to better their lot by individual acquisition of land or by union organization, they also used other means to that end. In South Carolina, for example, they formed cooperative associations to purchase plantations; the land was then distributed among the members to work on their own. In Wilmington, Del., and Washington, D.C., Negroes pooled their savings to establish small factories, producing such staples as household utensils, tobacco, and cigars, which furnished employment to themselves and other Negroes. The most notable example of this type of self-help was the Chesapeake Marine Railroad and Dry Dock Company, organized in 1865 by the indefatigable Isaac Myers as an answer to white shipyard workers who were driving Negroes out of the Baltimore shipyards. Capitalized at $40,000 and employing more than 300 Negro mechanics, the enterprise paid off its loans within five years and prospered for more than a decade, when finally the long depression after the Panic of 1873 posed problems too great for its management, as it did for many white enterprises.

The soil from which such ventures grew was thrift—a trait which few whites then or now associated with the Negro. But just as white workers in Britian and the United States somehow squeezed out of their poverty a few pennies a week to deposit in savings societies and dime banks, so did countless Negroes.

The success of a bank established for freedmen in Beaufort, S.C., in

1864, and of the deposit banks set up for soldiers by the army, prompted white friends of the Negro to seek a permanent institution which would promote and protect Negro savings. Led by John W. Alvord, an official of the Freedmen's Bureau, they obtained from Congress in 1865, a charter for the Freedmen's Savings and Trust Company, limited to Negro business and to investment of deposits in securities of the Federal Government. Included among its officials, in addition to Alvord, were such distinguished figures as Chief Justice Salmon P. Chase; William Cullen Bryant, the eminent poet and editor of the influential New York *Evening Post*; and Gerrit Smith, George L. Stearns, and Edward Atkinson—redoubtable abolitionists and successful businessmen.

Such sponsorship in itself recommended the bank to Negroes, but since the bank was chartered by Congress and its most notable executive was Alvord, who was especially active in promoting branches in the South, Negroes assumed it was a federal agency, with all the resources of the government behind it. Agents of the Freedmen's Bureau did little to correct this misconception. As a result, the savings of thousands of Negroes flowed to the bank. By March 1, 1866, deposits reached $305,000; three years later they were in excess of $7,257,000; by 1871 nearly $20 million was on deposit. Such success led to the bank's undoing.

White bankers, jealous of its progress and now eager to get Negro funds, withheld cooperation. Southern state governments, reflecting the section's old fear of a national banking system, opposed the bank on grounds that it took money away from local communities. Planters, seeing in it a threat to their hold over the sharecroppers, and viewing it as an appendage to the hated Freedmen's Bureau, used their power to block its expansion.

More important, the increasing wealth of the bank attracted attention from Northern speculators, particularly Jay Cooke, then engaged in his scheme to build a transcontinental railroad linking the Great Lakes with Puget Sound. Since the luminaries who lent their names to the bank paid little attention to its operations, it was possible for the speculators to get from Congress in 1870 an amendment to the bank's charter permitting it to invest part of its assets in notes and bonds secured by real estate mortgages. This opened the way for loans to speculators—Cooke's company borrowed a half-million dollars. Cooke and the First National Bank of Washington then obtained control of the bank, and held it until 1873, when Cooke's bankruptcy ushered in the Panic.

Immediately the Freedmen's Bank was in difficulty, for many of its "assets" consisted of loans to Cooke. A run on the bank began. In an effort to restore confidence in the institution, bank officials persuaded Frederick Douglass to assume the presidency, but when he discovered that he had to use his own funds to meet claims, he too "began to doubt the soundness of the bank." By midsummer of 1874 the bank was in such straits that Congress closed it.

In view of the close ties of the bank with the Federal Government, one might have expected some kind of aid to the depositors. As E. Merton Coulter has pointed out, considerations of morals, sound public policy, and help to the Negro surely called for repayment of the losses to depositors—but nothing was done.[1] When liquidation was finished, the thrifty black savers had to be content with sharing 62 per cent of the bank's assets of nearly $3,300,000.

It would be misleading to leave an impression of unrelieved poverty and failure. Despite the unfavorable circumstances, some Negroes did well. The wealthy communities of New Orleans and Charleston, for example, continued to prosper—perhaps even more than before, since they were now able to invest in railroad and street car companies and to use their new-found political power to promote their economic interests, just as whites were doing all over the nation. Negro depositors in Charleston had $125,000 in white-managed banks by 1876, despite the collapse of the Freedmen's Bank. In Georgia, Negroes owned $6,158,000 in taxable property in 1874, most of it obtained after the war. We have noted previously how black men acquired land in a number of other Southern states.

Some individuals even acquired "fortunes"—although compared to the millions being amassed by white tycoons of the period they appear miniscule. A South Carolina black planter was noteworthy because he was worth at least $15,000; a hotel keeper in Albany, N.Y., accumulated $60,000, and a barber in Missouri, $40,000. Most Negroes who prospered were in the professions or in business: doctors, dentists, lawyers, wood and coal merchants, builders, haulers, barbers. One business had a national reputation in its day: the Noisette nurseries of South Carolina.

But these were exceptions. The overwhelming mass of black men remained propertyless laborers.

[1] E. Merton Coulter, *The South During Reconstruction, 1865–1877* (Baton Rouge: Louisiana State University Press, 1947), pp. 88–89.

CHAPTER 3

Black Mind, Black Spirit

While rural and urban blacks tried to fight their way up from poverty, largely unsuccessfully, they fought, more successfully, to escape from ignorance, and to establish a sense and center of Negro community. The school and the church became prime instruments through which the Negro sought to find meaning in freedom. The obstacles he had to overcome, while less formidable than those in economic relations, were nevertheless impressive. A glance at white Southern society of the time will give us some perspective on them.

That society, as we have seen, was characterized by unprecedented fluidity, marked by the tensions to which rapid changes in social relations give rise. Not only did the native white have to learn to live with the Negro as free man—he also had to adjust himself to swiftly changing relationships between people of his own race. "New men" with money were unceremoniously making their way up the ladder, elbowing and gouging the traditional planters and yeomen out of their way. Squeezed by lack of capital, unfamiliar with the new ways of business, and ill at ease in this unfamiliar situation, the men bred to the ways of an older day were slipping downward.

Yankees, bustling with energy and sure of the rightness of their alien way of life, added to the changes and the tensions. They went South in increasing numbers, as missionaries, teachers, Freedmen's Bureau agents, soldiers, promoters, businessmen—bent on reshaping Southern society in accord with the American Dream of equality or on taking advantage of Southern distress to turn a fast buck. While some dedicated themselves to education and philanthropy, others established themselves in business in the towns or went into cotton planting by buying plantations at a fraction of their worth—and some contrived

55

to combine business and philanthropy. Whatever their motives or character, the Yankees constituted a new and abrasive element in Southern life.

It is not surprising that, caught up in this bewildering current of change, many native whites should feel insecure and that this feeling should manifest itself in hostility. Failing to grasp the basic causes of their distress, and prevented by law and custom from venting their hostility against other Southern whites, these native whites found the ideal scapegoat in the black man.

The Negro now was seen not simply as a symbol of defeat. As free citizen he was also seen as a menace to Anglo-Saxon civilization. Freed from the restraints of slavery and presumably lusting after white women, the Negro was readily pictured as threatening the supposedly genetic superiority of the white race. (A picture all the more readily accepted because a few Southern white women *had* intermarried with prosperous Negroes.) Thus arose the "rape syndrome," which explains some of the white savagery toward Negroes during and after Reconstruction. Needless to say, the effectiveness of the syndrome in uniting whites, transcending all lines of social cleavage, did not escape the notice of political demagogues or of businessmen bent on keeping white as well as black labor "in its place."

In this context it is noteworthy that the Negro, with the aid of Northern and Southern whites who espoused his cause, did make progress in education and in establishing his own center of community, the Negro church.

To many whites the idea of Negro education was a fantasy. J. D. B. DeBow, long time editor of the powerful *DeBow's Review* of New Orleans, found it laughable; Southerners, he said, were "accustomed to the idea that the Negroes are pretty stupid." Robert E. Lee thought the Negro not "as capable of acquiring knowledge as the white man is." Others shared the view of the Paducah, Kentucky, *Herald* that even to teach the black man "merely to read and write" was "to ruin him as a laborer." Perhaps even worse, Negro education was seen as a cover for Republican party propaganda. Both in the North and South there was fear that education, especially integrated education, would lead to "social equality," by which was signified the dread prospect of intermarriage. Whites in both sections, moreover, had a strong aversion to paying taxes to keep black youngsters in school.

Those who sought a rationale found it in the belief that at no time in history had black people produced a really civilized society. In Africa, their native continent, they had remained barbarians, while all around them other [and white] peoples had developed high civilizations. Indeed, the argument went, no more could be expected of Negroes. They were by nature (i.e., genetically) capable of only very limited intellectual attainment, and that only during childhood; at puberty, the physical senses became dominant. (A belief that strongly colored white attitudes toward integrated education.)

This rationale was by no means confined to the white South. It was generally accepted in the North and in Western Europe. It found classic expression in a letter written in 1863 by Louis Agassiz, the world-renowned scientist, born in Switzerland, educated at Heidelberg and Munich, and then embarked on his great career at Harvard. Wrote Agassiz:

> We should beware how we give to the blacks rights, by virtue of which they may endanger the progress of the whites before their temper has been tested by a prolonged experience. Social equality I deem at all times impracticable,—a natural impossibility, from the very character of the negro race. . . . We know of the existence of the negro race, with all its physical peculiarities, from the Egyptian monuments, . . . Upon these monuments the negroes are so represented as to show that in natural propensities and mental abilities they were pretty much what we find them at the present day,—indolent, playful, sensual, imitative, subservient, good-natured, versatile, unsteady in their purpose, devoted and affectionate. . . . Originally found in Africa, the negroes seem at all times to have presented the same characteristics wherever they have been brought into contact with the white race; . . . While Egypt and Carthage grew into powerful empires and attained a high degree of civilization; while in Babylon, Syria, and Greece were developed the highest culture of antiquity, the negro race groped in barbarism and *never originated a regular organization among themselves.* This is important to keep in mind, and to urge upon the attention of those who ascribe the condition of the modern negro wholly to the influence of slavery. . . .[1]

White friends of the Negro retorted that it was their duty as Christians and Americans to rescue the black man from ignorance: *that* much at least was owed him for two centuries of neglect. As Christians, they had an obligation to uplift his morals—especially sexual, which the Yankees found offensive; as Americans, they must train the freedman in the duties of citizenship. True, education of Negroes presented prob-

---

[1] Quoted in James Ford Rhodes, *History of the United States from the Compromise of 1850 to the Final Restoration of Home Rule in the South in 1877* (New York: The Macmillan Company, 1906), VI, 38.

lems. Some were bright, others were slow to learn; and in the area of morals many proved insensitive to marital obligations. But the problems, said the Yankee teachers, were due to social conditioning—the legacy of slavery—not to biological inheritance. Comparing Negroes to Irish immigrants in New England, they concluded that if the Irish could be taught then certainly the black men could be educated.

Other, and perhaps more hard-headed, Northerners, typified by Edward A. Atkinson, the New England abolitionist and textile company official, argued that education would develop habits of sobriety, frugality, industry, and thrift which would at once demonstrate the wisdom of abolition, provide Northern manufacturers with cheap cotton from free (rather than slave) labor, and open up for Northern merchants expanding markets among a thriving Negro citizenry.

Some Negroes wanted education on equally pragmatic grounds. The National Negro Labor Union, in 1869, pointed out that "educated labor is more productive and commands higher wages" than illiterate, while a Negro educational convention meeting in Louisville, Kentucky, that year advised Negroes to take advantage of educational opportunities to learn trades. Two years later the NNLU called on Congress to provide a national system of schools which would at once get rid of racial discrimination and provide an expanding pool of trained artisans through technical training.

This emphasis on federal responsibility reflected a trend in Negro thinking of the time. A national convention, meeting in January, 1869, saw in the schools already established by private philanthropy and the Freedmen's Bureau, "a feeble but honest acknowledgment of a great debt justly due and of long standing, contracted by centuries of ignorance, for which, unhappily, no adequate atonement can be made though the whole South were now covered with schoolhouses and supplied with teachers by a tax levied upon the property of the whole nation." In Illinois, Negroes asserted education was a right of citizenship, sealed by "the services of black soldiers in defending the liberties of the entire people." Alabama Negroes pointed out that education of the blacks would benefit the nation as a whole by providing training for citizenship, emphasizing that, "In a Republic, education is especially necessary, as the ignorant are always liable to be led astray by the arts of the demagogue."

In reference to the white outcry against taxation to support Negro education, Negroes replied that education was a public responsibility and that in many areas, both North and South, Negroes were taxed to support public schools from which their children were excluded. They also pointed out that, in the border states and Florida, Negro schools were supported only to the extent of special taxes levied against Negroes in addition to their usual taxes. This expanded a precedent set by Congress in 1862 when it set aside 10 per cent of taxes paid by Negro residents of the District of Columbia for support of Negro schools. In some places, at least, whites operated on the principle that education of Negroes should be a charge against the Negro community—not against the community as a whole.

Black response to what Congressman Richard H. Cain of South Carolina called the "great bugaboo" of "social equality" took two forms. One, expressed by Cain himself, was that social relationships between individuals were a personal matter. Negroes, said he, did not want social equality; wryly putting the white argument in a Negro framework, he asked his fellow Congressmen, "Do you suppose I would introduce into my family a class of white men I see in this country?" And he answered his question, "No, sir." The other view, put forth by Senator Hiram R. Revels of Mississippi, was that common education of whites and blacks would not lead to social relationships between them. Experience in New England, he said, showed that while children of both races mingled happily in school they pursued their separate social existences outside of it.

As for their educability, Negroes had no doubt. They swarmed into the schools in such numbers and with such intensity of interest as to astound the teachers. As Booker T. Washington recalled in what is now a famous passage: "It was a whole race trying to go to school. Few were too young, and none too old, to make the attempt to learn. As fast as any kind of teachers could be secured, not only were day-schools filled, but night schools as well. . . . Day schools, night schools, and Sunday schools were always crowded, and often many had to be turned away for want of room." Much later, DuBois pointed out that such a response was unusual in an ignorant and degraded people. Usually such people accept illiteracy as their lot, exalt their "folk wisdom" over formal education, and show distrust of "book learning"—as indeed did the poor whites of the South, who often shunned the opportunities afforded them by the new school systems set up by the Reconstruction governments. In Virginia, for example, whites were so apathetic that an indignant editor exhorted parents to support the schools "to prevent our white children from being outstripped in the race for intelligence by their sable competitors."

The campaign of education, to which Negroes so eagerly responded, began almost as soon as "contrabands" began showing up in Union army lines. Since neither military nor civilian administrators had plans to cope with the physical, far less the intellectual and spiritual, needs of the blacks, the work was taken over by the American Missionary Association, abolitionist in outlook and Congregationalist in inspiration. Its first school, opened at Fortress Monroe, Virginia, in September, 1861, was headed by Mary Peake, a black teacher. The initial efforts proved so successful that the AMA expanded its activities throughout the South as Union forces occupied Confederate territory. With financial backing from Northern churches and the benevolent cooperation of the Freedmen's Bureau, the AMA was able to report 528 teachers in the South by 1867.

Other religious groups followed suit, mainly Methodists, Baptists, and Presbyterians, bent on "saving souls" but aware that to do so they must first dispel ignorance. Aiding in the effort were many Northern Negro organizations: black Methodists through their churches—the African Methodist Episcopal and African Methodist Episcopal Zion—black Baptists, and various secular organizations, such as the African Civilization Society, which set up schools for blacks in Washington. Compared to white, the resources of the Negro churches were slim indeed. Even so, the African Methodist Episcopal organization gave nearly $167,000 for aid to Southern Negroes between 1862 and 1868.

Another approach was taken by secular Freedmen's Aid Societies, principally those of Boston, New York, and Philadelphia, usually organized and led by Unitarians. In 1862, a band of abolitionists, including recent graduates of Harvard, Yale, and Brown, and a brilliant young Negro teacher, Charlotte Forten, granddaughter of the famous Negro abolitionist, James Forten, went to Beaufort, S.C. They were implementing a plan of Edward L. Pierce, young Boston abolitionist, to take over plantations deserted by their owners and use them to train Negroes in the ways of freedom and to demonstrate both that blacks would work without compulsion and that free labor would prove more productive and progressive than slave.

Such an experiment, it was believed, would lay bare the problems and possibilities of Reconstruction in the South as a whole—and also prod the Lincoln Administration toward emancipation. An indispensable condition for success was to prove the educability of the Negro. In this case it was the more difficult because the Sea Island blacks, thanks to their geographical isolation, were among the most backward of slaves and their dialect was almost incomprehensible to the newcomers. Miss Forten, on first encountering them, thought them "the most dismal specimens I ever saw."

The experiment proved sufficiently successful for the Freedmen's Aid Societies to enlarge their programs; by 1866 they maintained 760 teachers in the South. Thereafter secular, if not religious, Northern philanthropic interest in the blacks declined. During their active years the societies spent nearly $3,000,000 on education, involving about 150,000 black pupils.

Still another source of education for the Negro was the Union Army. The black regiments were almost entirely illiterate; white officers found it an essential part of their duty to teach black noncommissioned officers how to write and figure. In this they were aided by Negro chaplains and those soldiers who could read and write. "School tents" were set up in all Negro outfits, through which thousands of blacks received their introduction to education. Many of the instructors were abolitionists, who combined teaching the "three R's" with what today we would call political education. Col. James Beecher, brother of the more famous Henry Ward Beecher, "neglected no opportunity to form schools of instruction for his men, in order that they might become not only intelligent, efficient soldiers, but also intelligent, self-respecting citizens."

The Army's efforts were not confined to soldiers. In Louisiana, General Nathaniel Banks, who had aroused abolitionist opposition with his policy of hiring out freedmen to planters at a maximum wage of ten dollars a month and under conditions reminiscent of slavery, blunted some of the criticism with his educational program. In March, 1864, he appointed a special board to organize a school system for the blacks financed from taxes the board was empowered to levy. Two abolitionists headed the program. By July, 1865, 126 schools were open, with 230 teachers and 15,000 pupils; an additional 5,000 adults were taught in night and Sunday classes. In Mississippi, Superintendent John Eaton, disturbed by friction between representatives of the American Missionary Association and the Freedmen's Aid societies, and corruption among some teachers, finally won authority to take over the schools already established. He abolished tuition fees for children of destitute parents, raised standards, and set up more efficient administration. The schools flourished: before Appomattox there were 30 operating in the Vicksburg and Natchez areas, with 60 teachers and nearly 4,400 pupils.

A measure of order was introduced with the advent of the Freedmen's Bureau. Although it had no educational responsibilities when established, the bureau quickly found it could not avoid them in executing its task of aiding the freedmen. Since the religious and philanthropic agencies in the field afforded the best means of reaching the Negroes, the bureau aided them by providing rations, quarters, and transportation for teachers and government buildings for schools. Funds for this purpose were derived from rental of abandoned properties. The act of July, 1866, authorized the bureau to carry on its own educational work as well as collaborating with private organizations. An appropriation of $521,000 for school purposes was provided, to be supplemented by revenue from sale of Confederate government property. Under the direction of John W. Alvord, its Superintendent of Education and a veteran abolitionist, the bureau spent $5,200,000 on education by 1870. In July of that year it operated 4,239 schools throughout the South, with 9,300 teachers and over 247,000 pupils, most of whom were Negroes.

These expenditures represented only half the cost of maintaining schools. The remainder was financed by Northern religious and philanthropic organizations—and by the freedmen themselves, who out of their poverty contributed $785,000. This testimony of black faith in education was confirmed by whites active in the field. Plantation superintendents in the Sea Islands reported the most effective means of discipline was the threat to take away school books from the field hands! Dr. Joseph Warren, General Superintendent of Education for the Army Department of Mississippi, noted that difficulties there were such as "would be seriously in the way of educating any class of people. Only an enthusiastic desire for improvement could lead any people to put forth the efforts which the freed people are making to procure instruction."

But the desire to learn and the ability to learn are two different matters: were the Negroes able to learn? Teachers almost universally agreed that Negroes learned to read as rapidly and as well as whites and excelled in subjects where rote memory was required. In writing and in subjects which called for abstract thought, such as mathematics, they did not measure up to white standards of achievement, a situation which most teachers realistically attributed to the background of slavery. But the motivation to learn was there: adults as well as children went to school, and parents who could not attend were often tutored by their children. As E. L. Pierce commented, if whites did as well "under such adverse circumstances, they would be regarded as prodigies." [2]

There were many such circumstances. White hostility to "nigger schools" was manifest practically everywhere. In Florida, the Superintendent of Education reported in 1866 that whites entertained a "deadly hatred" toward black education. In Georgia, that same year, teachers were beaten and school buildings burned.

Even among his friends, the black man had difficulties. He became a bone of contention in the bitter institutional rivalries of Northern

---

[2] Quoted in James M. McPherson, *The Struggle for Liberty: Abolitionists and the Negro in the Civil War and Reconstruction* (Princeton: Princeton University Press, 1964), p. 164.

benevolent societies, religious and secular alike. Also, many of the societies' schools charged fees—an effective barrier against the poor. In some places, the fees were pocketed by corrupt teachers. Other teachers, honest but lacking in empathy, displayed conventional white attitudes of contempt or condescension in relations with their pupils.

And the blacks had problems of their own. The wandering of families during the post-war years made school attendance uncertain, if not impossible, for thousands of Negro children. Other youngsters, whose labor was needed in the fields, also found schooling difficult to obtain—although enterprising teachers in some areas coped with this by scheduling classes during leisure time. Those who were able to attend had obstacles to overcome, too. Pupils often had to care for younger children while at school; sometimes several different classes were held simultaneously in one big room; and the language and pictures of the textbooks were those of an alien world. Nevertheless, the Negro was determined to master the mysteries of reading, writing, and figuring: without such mastery, freedom was meaningless.

At first, the Negro passion for education had little counterpart among whites. Of the 111,000 pupils registered in Freedmen's Aid society schools on June 30, 1867, only 1,300 were white. Apart from indifference or hostility to education itself among many poorer whites, there was general community opposition to the schools which made itself felt in rigorous social ostracism of parents and youngsters who participated. This prevented many parents from sending youngsters to school, and in some cases forced them to withdraw children already enrolled.

White resentment centered on the fact that the schools were "mixed," desegregated. Also, it was charged, teachers taught Republican politics and "social equality." If they did not preach the latter openly, it was said, they taught it the more effectively through example. That most of the teachers were Yankees also contributed to native white suspicion, although most bitter feeling was directed at those who were Southern born. White churchmen, believing that the post-war South was in the hands of the ungodly, and vexed at the invasion of their religious domain by Northern missionaries, inveighed against the schools. In Columbus, Georgia, one minister persuaded black clergymen to join his campaign, arguing that the Yankee teachers stirred up race prejudice. In Louisville a teacher was denied admission to a Baptist church because she refused to give up her work in a mission school. In some areas the teachers were tolerated, but in most communities they were shunned by local whites, and in places where feeling ran especially high, teachers were assaulted and school houses burned.

There were whites, however, who perceived that the pre-war educational system was out of keeping with the needs of the post-war South. Such as it was, the system had served the interests of the wealthy minority, kept the masses largely illiterate, and, in the words of General Daniel H. Hill of North Carolina, provided in plenty "orators and statesmen, but did nothing to enrich us, nothing to promote material greatness." The emphasis now, he said, must be, not on "the everlasting twaddle about politics" but on "the practical and the useful." The South must provide for itself artisans, mechanics, engineers, and scientists as well as traditional scholars in the classics.

Such men, however, thought entirely in terms of white education. The idea that there might emerge a great black scientist, like George Washington Carver, was quite beyond the reach of their imaginations, just as the work of Benjamin Banneker, the astronomer who counted Thomas Jefferson among his admirers, and Elijah McCoy, who perfected a method of lubricating engines while in operation, was beyond their ken. Their thinking, as well as general native white attitudes, was reflected in the educational legislation passed by Johnson governments.

Such legislation provided public schools for white youngsters only. The Negro schools that were permitted depended on funds coming from Negro taxpayers, who, of course, also had to contribute to the maintenance of white schools. Even so, the new public school systems were weak: the traditional aristocratic view of education as the prerogative of an elite did not die overnight; there was much white apathy; insufficient funds were voted; and, naturally, there was black opposition.

The first real commitment of the South to unrestricted public education supported by general taxation came with the Reconstruction governments. Three groups combined to bring this about: native whites who saw that the future of the South, and particularly the future of the white South, depended on a modern school system; Northerners, who believed in public education in principle and who were convinced that only a public system could afford schooling to the blacks; and blacks themselves, who held education to be a matter of right and perceived its role in their future progress. Dominating the conventions called to write new state constitutions in accordance with the Reconstruction acts, representatives of these groups wrote into the new instruments of government provisions for free public school systems open to all children, regardless of race. Only in North Carolina was attendance made compulsory.

The prickly question of segregation was left open. Most states, though under Republican control, established separate white and black schools. Only Louisiana and South Carolina required integration—but in the former only the New Orleans schools were mixed and in the latter only the State University was integrated. The Peabody Education Fund threw its weight on the side of the segregationists by refusing to make grants to mixed schools. The consequent neglect of Negro education, especially after Conservatives gained control of various states in the early 70's, led to Negro demands for federal legislation outlawing discrimination in the schools.

A Civil Rights Convention in 1873, in reference to legislation then pending, called upon Congress to assure that the "common school, paid for and owned by all citizens in common, shall not be made to serve to the degradation and humiliation of any class thereof." Indeed, discrimination against Negro children was so patent that when Congress took up what became the famous Civil Rights Act of 1875 the bill contained a clause designed to end segregated schools. There was an immediate outcry from native whites, some of whom held it was "better to have no schools than mixed schools."

They had a powerful ally and spokesman in a Yankee, Barnas Sears, former Baptist clergyman and president of Brown University, now general agent for the prestigious Peabody Education Fund, established in 1867 to upgrade Southern education without arousing the opposition of native whites. Believing that integrated education was a "shadowy abstraction" that would impose "popular ignorance upon the South," and with the prestige and millions of the Peabody Fund behind him, Sears was able to persuade President Grant and Congressman Benjamin F. Butler of Massachusetts, a manager of the bill, to drop the provision.

This failure points up a larger failure: the refusal of the nation as a whole to face up to its responsibilities to the South, both white and black. Apart from the problem of race, the basic issue was economic. The impoverished South, still recovering from the war, did not possess the resources to support a modern school system, let alone the dual system it was fostering. To provide such resources was an aim of the Peabody Fund and other philanthropies, but in view of the magnitude of the problem they were inadequate. As Senator Henry W. Blair of New Hampshire put it, they furnished "dew" when "heavy rains" were needed. The "rains" he had in mind were federal funds, to be disbursed to states in proportion to their illiteracy. Other measures providing for federal aid to education were introduced by Rep. George F. Hoar of Massachusetts and Senator W. T. Willey of West Virginia. All had some measure of legislative success, all were supported by Negro Senators and Congressmen, but none passed. White and black Southerners were left to find—and fund—their own way.

The way was not easy. Some whites, agreeing with the Southern leaders who were calling for a new and more practical approach to education, were eager to have their children go to school. Generally, however, poorer whites looked upon schooling as an upper-class luxury, too expensive for them to indulge in. More prosperous whites, overlooking the fact that Negroes and their poorer white neighbors also paid taxes, resented taxation to pay for other people's children. Nearly all objected to using public funds for Negro education. Negroes, however, insisted on their right to schooling, and through exercise of their political power were able to get it, to a degree.

There were other problems: violence, poor teachers and administrators, corruption, and diversion of funds to other public purposes.

In Mississippi in 1870–71, poor white farmers, aroused by charges that school taxation for Negroes would further impoverish them and that the newly established public schools were used to propagate Republican political doctrines and ideas of social equality, went on a rampage of arson and murder in eight counties, burning school houses and torturing and killing teachers. As a result, by the summer of 1871 some counties had no schools in operation. The Mississippi outbreak was exceptional only in its virulence. Elsewhere in Southern states the violence was more restrained: teachers were threatened and beaten; in many instances school houses were burned. Most of the violence was directed, of course, against black schools and the teachers in black schools, and it was sporadic rather than systematic.

Such outrages, coupled with the more usual social ostracism and increasing disillusionment with their tasks, led many Northern teachers and administrators to leave the South. Others were discouraged from entering by low salaries, uncertainty of tenure, and the frequent reports of violence which appeared in Northern newspapers. In the words of J. C. DeGrees, State Superintendent of Schools in Texas, "Few persons have the nerve to meet the continual insults, the social ostracism, the threats of injury, and all the annoyances to which the teachers of colored schools are subjected."

The need for teachers was met in part by graduates of mission colleges and normal schools established by Northern philanthropy, but even they did not produce trained administrators. The new state school systems, therefore, often made do with poorly trained teachers and even more poorly trained administrators; often such teachers and administrators obtained appointment through politicians and regarded their jobs as political rewards. The effect of such a situation on education needs no elaboration.

The school systems were also endangered in another way. Funds raised (by taxes) for school purposes provided easy pickings for office holders with easy consciences. Perhaps more dangerous was the habit of hard-pressed state governments of diverting school moneys to meet other expenses, as happened in Georgia, North Carolina, South Carolina, Alabama, and Louisiana. In the last, an entire million dollars in school bonds was used to pay the expenses of the legislature in 1872. Diversion of moneys in counties was equally rife. This was nothing new in Southern experience, however: the public school systems set up early in the nineteenth century in Tennessee and Virginia had never functioned effectively largely because school funds were devoted to other purposes.

Thus, school systems inadequately financed to begin with, were straitened still further. When Democrats, who usually styled themselves "Conservatives," regained control in individual states, school budgets became a prime target. In 1869, the new administration in Tennessee repealed the compulsory school law and left public education to the option of the counties; except in Memphis and Nashville all Negro schools were closed. The following year, the Conservative governor of Virginia announced that the property tax levied for education would not be enforced. In Georgia, alleged shortage of funds led to closing all schools in 1872; the same situation was repeated in Arkansas in 1874. Promising beginnings in North Carolina and Mississippi were abruptly halted when new administrations drastically slashed salaries of teachers and school administrators and otherwise forced economies which resulted in the closing of many schools. Negro schools, of course, bore the brunt of such measures.

Paradoxically, the pressure on Negro education was in part the result of an increasing white appreciation of the value of education—for white children—an attitude which even in Mississippi eventually made attacks on the schools "bad politics." As white demands rose in face of the tax squeeze, they could be met, if only in part, by transferring funds from Negro schools to white. Negro education might have been abandoned altogether had it not been for black political power; a growing feeling among influential whites that some Negro education was a good thing (if done on native white terms); and continued, if sadly diminished, Northern interest in the freedman, symbolized by the presence of schools supported by Northern churches.

If Negro education was regarded with doubt in the white South, it was also suspect in the white North. Not until the 1850's had some Northern states—Ohio, Michigan, Wisconsin, Iowa—provided public funds for Negro schools. In some states, such Negro education as was given was segregated. New York State authorized local school districts to establish segregated systems; Pennsylvania and Ohio required segregation when black pupils numbered more than twenty in any school district. Such schools anticipated the segregated schools of the South; they were inadequately financed, wretchedly housed, and often poorly staffed. In some places, school boards made no effort to provide any type of Negro schooling, segregated or otherwise.

Northern blacks fought such conditions. They built and financed their own schools where necessary—and where they had the funds. They demanded public education on an integrated basis; and, if that were not possible, separate school systems, providing these were not only separate but *actually* equal. On occasion, as in Hartford, Conn., and Rochester, N.Y., they felt compelled to call for separate schools because of maltreatment of black children in integrated schools.

The Northern white attitudes which lay behind educational discrimination were little changed by the war. Doubts were expressed of Negro educability. Taxpayers protested white support of black schooling. And parents almost universally feared that mixed education would lead to racial amalgamation. White children, reflecting the feelings of their elders, insulted and abused black children—and then their parents used the incidents to call for exclusion of the blacks, for the black youngsters' own good and safety. A Negro editor in 1872, noting the process, commented, "so great has been the solicitude of some for the welfare of our children that they would sooner deprive them of all means of education than subject them to abuse from white children."

Another example of white rationalization of segregation is to be seen in the report of the Illinois superintendent of public instruction in 1870. In that year the state constitutional convention committed Illinois to providing education for all children, but leaving uncertain whether or not it was to be segregated. The issue should not be agitated, said the superintendent, for "It is one of those matters which involves no *principle* worth striving about, and which are best left to regulate themselves."

He followed with advice to Negroes:

> What our colored citizens need, . . . , is the means of educating their children; . . . not the paltry privilege, . . . of sitting in the same seats, or in the same house, with white children. This great right to free education they now enjoy, . . . Let them make the most of it, and become an upright, intelligent, educated people, and all other questions and consequences will take care of themselves. . . .

In fact, said he, there was no need to be aroused over segregation, because the obvious economic burden of maintaining separate school systems would soon put an end to it: ". . . *Prejudice* and *cost* will be the two antagonistic forces . . . and sooner or later the latter will be likely to prevail. When the continued indulgence of a mere prejudice is found to be expensive, it is not probable that it will be very long persisted in . . ." (Italics in original.)

The superintendent was too optimistic about the beneficent operation of economic forces: in 1874 he confessed that in many instances local school trustees simply ignored education of Negro children. A similar situation existed in neighboring Indiana.

Northern courts, in fact, upheld segregation in principle. In 1874 the Illinois Supreme Court (*Chase vs. Stephenson*), while ordering integration in a case involving only four black children, made it plain that had there been a sufficient number of blacks in the school district to make separate and equal schools economically feasible, its decision might well have been different. That same year the California Supreme Court, in *Ward vs. Flood*, ordered admission of Negro youngsters to white public schools but only because the school district involved had made no provision for "separate schools . . . actually maintained for the education of colored children." In short, if in a given school district there was a sufficient number of black children to justify separate schools and if such schools were in fact provided, black children legally had no access to white schools.

Under the circumstances—given the limited resources of Northern philanthropy, white hostility to Negro education, increasing emphasis on white as opposed to Negro schools, opposition in North and South to integrated schools, and the critical state of the Southern economy, and indeed of the national economy after 1873—it is perhaps not surprising that progress was slow. Illiteracy among Negroes fell at the rate of about one percent per year, from over 90 per cent in 1860 to nearly 80 per cent in 1870 and to 70 per cent in 1880. That even this much was accomplished was due largely to the black determination to learn, despite all obstacles. Sir George Campbell, the British traveler in the South during Reconstruction, noted that "the blacks are very anxious to learn—more so than the lower whites." That this was no ephemeral situation is indicated by Ray Stannard Baker's finding nearly 30 years later: "The eagerness of the colored people for a chance to send their children to school is . . . astonishing and pathetic. They will submit to all sorts of inconveniences in order that the children may get an education."

But what kind of education did the Negroes want, other than learning to read, write, and figure? Most whites, if they believed in Negro education at all, wanted it confined to "industrial" or vocational training. The National Negro Labor Union never ceased to exhort its members on the value of such training. But there was a significant difference in their objectives. While whites favored "industrial" education as a means of keeping the Negro "in his place," Negroes wanted it to be a means of liberation, through which the black man could win a more substantial place in industry and as much economic independence as his white counterpart.

This conflict in aims was put succinctly by the *New National Era* in 1873, after some Northern journals had advised Negro parents to have their children trained for trades. This advice, said the Negro paper, was "like telling a man in the water with his hands and legs heavily ironed, to strike out manfully for the shore. Will the proprietors of . . . [the] journals accept a colored apprentice?" This, of course, was the nub of the matter. Given the attitudes of white employers and unions, where was a young Negro craftsman to find a place where he could use his skills?

Nevertheless, the appeal of vocational training for both whites and Negroes helps explain the success of such institutions as Hampton Institute, opened in 1868 by the American Missionary Association. Under the guidance of General Samuel C. Armstrong, the Hawaiian-born commander of Negro troops during the war, the Institute kept its costs —and fees—low by using student labor on a wide variety of tasks, thus affording them "on the job" training while providing a modicum of academic instruction. However, its major contribution, as was Tuskegee's later, was to provide trained teachers for the developing Southern school system. Indeed, genuine vocational education, except in housework and other such fields, was never seriously undertaken in Southern schools. It was too expensive—and white taxpayers had no intention of training competitors for white craftsmen.

There were also blacks and whites, however, who were not content with vocational education and its social implication of confining the Negro to roles of farmer and artisan, essential though those might be. These men, anticipating DuBois' advocacy of the cause of the "talented tenth," emphasized the crucial need for educated black leadership among a developing people. Such leadership would come largely from professional people, who in turn would be products of Southern adaptations of the classic liberal arts colleges of New England. As the historian of the AMA put it in 1909:

The fathers of forty years ago anticipated the criticism of later years as to the wisdom of colleges for the development of a backward race. So, they said, let it be granted that other lines of education are imperative; colleges also certainly are needed, . . . Thorough training, large knowledge, and the best culture possible are needed to invigorate, direct, purify, and broaden life; needed for the wise administration of citizenship, . . .

Related to this was a growing realization among Northern abolitionists and philanthropists that their resources were quite inadequate to cope with the demands of expanding Negro education at all levels. They came to feel that such funds as were available might best be used to develop centers for the training of teachers and others on a liberal arts as opposed to a vocational level.

Various Northern religious denominations, most notably Congregationalists, Methodists, and Baptists, added strength to the college movement. They sought to promote a trained native black ministry and to cultivate what they hoped would be a growing body of black professional people which would lend substance to the denomination's growth in the South. Such colleges as they founded, however, tended to be doctrinal in emphasis rather than devoted to liberal education.

The record of the several bodies in those early years is impressive. Between 1866 and 1869 the American Missionary Association established seven colleges, including what are now Fisk and Atlanta universities, and it helped the Freedmen's Bureau open Howard University in 1867. Religious denominations also were active, so that by 1879 there were 39 normal schools, colleges, and theological seminaries throughout the South supported by Northern groups. Among the more notable were Straight University in New Orleans (Congregational), Claflin University in South Carolina (Methodist), and what is now Morehouse College (Baptist) in Atlanta. Methodists also opened medical schools in Nashville and New Orleans, while the Baptists opened one in Raleigh, North Carolina.

Largely because of inadequate resources, Negro churches were slow to respond to Negro needs for higher education. Beginning in 1878, however, they too began to found their own colleges. In that year the Colored Methodists opened Lane College at Jackson, Tennessee; a year later, the African Methodist Episcopal Zion Church opened Livingstone College in North Carolina; and the African Methodist Episcopal Church a few years afterwards established Allen University at Columbia, South Carolina, and Morris Brown College in Atlanta.

Like many Northern colleges of the period, the new Southern colleges were little better than high schools, but that in itself was meeting a need when high schools were relatively uncommon even in the North. Not all of them survived. Insufficient funds, poor administration, widespread native white hostility, the declining interest of the North, especially after the economic collapse of 1873, and denominational rivalry —all took their toll.

Among those which did survive were such outstanding schools as Howard, Atlanta, and Fisk, which attained good academic repute not only in the South but also in the nation. Contributing to this was their development of elementary and secondary branches in order to provide themselves with qualified students—a striking commentary on the quality of public education for Negroes. This process, of course, tended to screen out the children of the poor—they lacked the necessary educational background and their parents lacked the necessary funds for fees. Thus, oriented to the small but growing black middle class and to those who had the means to attain middle class status, and staffed largely by Yankees who spread the gospel of industry, thrift, frugality, and sobriety, the colleges turned out hundreds of successful teachers, professional men, and businessmen.

The Yankees communicated more than the economic virtues. To them, the gospel of success was vitally linked to beliefs in human equality, political democracy, and nurture of the mind and spirit. Some practiced what they preached—and their students had the rare experience of being treated as men and women, not as Negroes. Thus, while the colleges produced graduates able to make their way successfully in the restricted areas of American life open to them, they also sparked in the graduates a deep dissatisfaction with the restrictions and a questioning of the society which enforced them. This Yankee contribution was accurately appraised by the racist demagogue of Mississippi, James K. Vardaman: "What the North is sending South is not money, but dynamite; this education is ruining our Negroes. They're demanding equality."

Some of the Negro graduates did indeed go on to become leaders in the long struggle for equality. Among the more famous were: W. E. B. DuBois, who did his undergraduate work at Fisk before he became Harvard's first Negro Ph.D.; James Weldon Johnson, Atlanta University graduate, who achieved fame as a writer and as a leader of the National Association for the Advancement of Colored People; and Carter G. Woodson, a student at Berea College in Kentucky when that institution was unique in the South as a bi-racial school—an experiment that the Kentucky legislature and the United States Supreme Court ordered stopped. Woodson, also a Harvard Ph.D., and a practicing historian, founded the Association for the Study of Negro Life and History and the *Journal of Negro History*, both designed to develop a sense of black worth and dignity by familiarizing American Negroes with their own past.

It was this aspect of the Southern Negro college which led DuBois to say that "this astonishing movement to plant the New England college in the South, and to give the Southern black man a leadership based on scholarship and character" proved to be "the salvation of the South and the Negro." To others, such as Booker T. Washington, this emphasis on academic education was both impractical and dangerous. It was impractical because most black men needed to be trained as farmers and mechanics, not as scholars; dangerous because it hindered them in the tricky business of peaceful co-existence with native whites. "Put down your buckets where you are!" admonished Washington in 1895, urging his fellow blacks to accommodate themselves to the ways of Southern whites. His white friend and supporter, William Henry Baldwin, the latter-day carpetbag executive of the Southern railway, struck more directly at the colleges in his counsel to Negroes: "Face the music; avoid social questions; leave politics alone; continue to be patient; live moral lives; live simply; learn to work, . . . learn that it is a mistake to be educated out of your environment."

This approach not only came to dominate the public schools; it also superseded the early emphasis on democracy and equality in many Negro colleges. Heavily dependent on Northern philanthropy, which shared the views of Washington and Baldwin, the Negro colleges, when the old guard of abolitionist teachers and administrators passed away, replaced them with whites and blacks committed to the philosophy of accommodation. But the thought and spirit of protest, tempered in the days of Reconstruction, while they might be muted for two generations, did not perish, as the struggle for civil rights in our day was to show.

Poor but ambitious blacks might have found opportunities in the state universities, had these been open to them, but the end of the Reconstruction governments came too swiftly for such a policy to become firmly established. In the interim, the universities were subjects of bitter contention between Republicans and Conservatives, usually over the issue of integration. Such friction led to the closing of the University of North Carolina, 1870–1875. Conservatives in Alabama, having driven out, through the medium of the Ku Klux Klan, a Northerner who was appointed president of the state university, closed the institution in 1871 and reopened it in accord with their segregationist policy. Louisiana State University was denied state funds from 1873 to 1877 because it refused to admit Negro students. In Arkansas, Republicans opened the state's first public university in 1872, open to both races. Only one Negro registered, and he was taught privately off campus. In Mississippi and South Carolina the story was somewhat different.

Republicans governing in Mississippi maintained the state university at Oxford as an all-white institution, but founded two schools for blacks only: Holly Springs Normal School and Alcorn University.

The former, designed to produce teachers, charged no tuition and paid students, who pledged themselves to become teachers, an allowance of 50 cents a week. In turn, students rented their books and paid board of $7.50–$9.00 a month. Starting with 50 students when it opened in 1870, the school had 134 by 1875. Its basic problem was financial: even under Republican auspices its appropriation never exceeded $5,000 a year, out of which had to be paid teachers' salaries, maintenance and operating expenses, and student aid, including the weekly allowance of 50 cents per student. When the Conservatives triumphed in 1875, the school was in danger. In 1877 appropriations were cut to $3,000 a year, in 1890 to $2,500. When James K. Vardaman, who thought education "ruined" Negroes, became governor in 1904, appropriations were cut off and the school closed.

If Alcorn University survived, it was largely because it was accommodationist in practice long before Booker T. Washington made accommodation into a policy. In its early days the institution reflected the concern of blacks and some whites in higher education for children of the poor. Out of an annual appropriation of $55,000—equal to that of the University of Mississippi—the school granted numerous scholarships and even free meals to impoverished students. Young Negroes came in large numbers, but many were ill-prepared. The trustees had chosen as president Hiram R. Revels, who in 1870 had taken Jefferson Davis' seat in the United States Senate. He was the first black man to serve in that body.

Revels, a "white man's Negro" of undoubted probity, who campaigned for the Conservatives in the 1875 elections, had no gift for administration. Revels, the faculty, and the trustees were soon embroiled in disputes, and Revels' endorsement of Democrats did not endear him to Republicans. After an investigation of his administration, the Republican legislature removed him in 1875. It also struck a blow at higher education for the poor by abolishing scholarships and free meals, and slashing the yearly appropriation to $15,000. Conservatives, taking power in 1876, cut appropriations even more, but restored Revels to office. Under him and his successors, according to Vernon Lane Wharton, who wrote a classic study of the Negro in Mississippi during the Reconstruction, the school was "quiet, unobtrusive, and uninspired." Which, of course, was precisely what native whites thought Negro schools should be.

In South Carolina the prospects for higher education seemed brighter and the integration issue more sharply joined than in Mississippi. An integrated South Carolina Agricultural College and Mechanics Institute was established in 1872 by the legislature and was made a state-supported part of Claflin University, a Methodist school. With generous appropriations, the institution flourished in training farmers, carpenters, blacksmiths, and other artisans. When Conservatives captured control, it was transformed into a segregated Negro college, still state-supported and still part of Claflin.

In the meantime, the Reconstruction legislature, having rejected proposals for setting up separate black and white state universities, banned segregation at the University of South Carolina (1869) and appointed Negroes to its board of regents. An experienced Northern administrator was named president, and in his regime a black man, Richard T. Greener, was appointed professor of mental and moral philosophy. Greener, who had made a distinguished record as the first Negro to graduate from Harvard College, also taught Greek, Latin, and American constitutional history.

Such developments, naturally, were deplored by native whites. Although no Negro actually registered until 1873, white students and faculty members began withdrawing as early as 1869; another exodus took place when the first Negro was accepted. Despite this, enrollment went up—from 65 in 1869 to 233 in 1875, of whom 90 per cent were Negroes. More than a third of the students received state scholarships —a reflection of the desire of South Carolina legislators not only to provide the conditions for an open society but also to stimulate the growth of leadership from among the poor of both races. This promising experiment, like many others, came to an end with the advent of Conservatives to power. The university was closed for three years and then re-opened as an all-white institution.

The Negro, then, made a beginning in education during Reconstruction. It was not much more than that in either the public schools or the state colleges—but a beginning was made. The value of Negro education was eventually accepted, however grudgingly and from whatever motive; and the commitments of the states to black schools were still inscribed in their constitutions long after Reconstruction was over. The commitments were all too often ignored, and they were never honored on a basis similar to that of white education—but they were never repudiated.

That the commitments could be met on less than honorable terms was hardly the fault of illiterate, poverty-stricken, and disfranchised blacks. These were impotent in the face of a solid white South backed by a white North which increasingly shared the native white view of the Negro and his potentialities. If, in the course of time, a new generation of black leaders arose in the twentieth century to launch a new crusade for equality and democracy, it was due not only to Northern colleges but also, and perhaps more significantly, to the Southern private schools and colleges, founded during Reconstruction, which for long kept alive in Southern blacks a sense of black worth and nurtured hope for a black future in white America.

Education, however eagerly sought after by blacks, was not *their* education. It was white education for Negroes. Many teachers were white, and the growing number of Negro teachers taught as they had been taught in white-directed normal schools or colleges. Textbooks, written by whites, drew their language and materials from white society, often the alien society of New England. Increasingly, however, texts came to reflect the values and attitudes of native white society as Conservative elements saw the importance of impressing upon children "an unbiased Southern point of view." Curricula, when not dominated by a Yankee "classical" outlook quite unsuitable for a people of farmers and artisans, were shaped to satisfy the feelings of native whites.

Even with the best of motives it was difficult for whites to avoid condescension toward those whom they considered "charges." Some Northern supporters of missionary schools tried to inculcate in teachers the principle that education of the freedmen "was the education of savages into self-governing men," and some teachers thought that more important than "book knowledge" were "needles and thread and soap and decent clothing." One Northern girl opposed integrated schools, for, she wrote, "as the blacks are now, their society would be degrading."

Thus the schoolhouse, which in any event touched only a minority of the Negro population, could never become a focus of black community. But the freedmen felt an imperative need for community. Few of them were received socially by whites, and in most such cases it was obviously for white business or political purposes. In addition, they felt native white hostility and Northern white patronage. Only within their own group were they accepted as human beings. A center was needed for self-expression, for freedom to be themselves, with their own chosen guides and leaders, free from white control, free from the all-pervasive white contempt or condescension. Such an institution was at hand—the "invisible institution" of slavery, the black church.

While some efforts to Christianize slaves had been made since the seventeenth century, it appears that in the South the Negro church had its origins in the Second Great Awakening, the religious revival which swept the country in the early years of the nineteenth century. In the South, Baptist and Methodist evangelists set out to convert the ungodly among poor whites, small planters and farmers, plantation overseers, free Negroes, and slaves. The well-to-do, who were generally Episcopalians, Congregationalists, or Presbyterians, were beyond their reach.

Among the free and slave blacks the evangelists were notably successful, "raising up" from among them many "exhorters" to preach the "Good News" of Christian redemption to their own people, and, on occasion, to whites. Redemption was viewed as a purely personal matter, not social: it came from individual dedication to God, exemplified in hard work, obedience (to one's master as well as one's God), abstinence from the things of the flesh, and "pure living." Such issues as slavery were irrelevant: salvation was concerned not with this world, but the next.

Further, redemption began with "conversion," usually a highly emotional personal experience undergone in the orgiastic setting of revivals or camp meetings, which were as popular and as effective among blacks as among whites. The climax of one such white meeting was described by a witness, Mrs. Frances Trollope, the famous and unpopular Englishwoman who traveled in the United States in the late 1820's:

> above a hundred persons, nearly all females, came forward, uttering howlings and groans so terrible that I shall never cease to shudder when I recall them. . . . On the word being given, "let us pray," they all fell on their knees; but this posture was soon changed for others that permitted greater scope for the convulsive movements of their limbs; and they were soon all lying on the ground. . . . They threw about their limbs with . . . incessant and violent motion, . . .
>
> But how am I to describe the sounds . . . ? I know no words which can convey an idea of it. Hysterical sobbings, convulsive groans, shrieks and screams the most appalling, burst forth on all sides. . . .

This was the kind of Christian religion in which the Southern Negro church originated: devoid of intellectual content, almost exclusively emotional in appeal, stripped of liturgy and hierarchy, emphasizing purely personal behavior as the way to redemption, and oriented to the hereafter rather than the here and now.

Such a religion, with its obvious utility as a means of social control, might have been expected to win acclaim from planters haunted by the dread of slave insurrections. But many were wary: emotional excess, while pardonable among Anglo-Saxons, was dangerous among blacks; the prominence to which some free Negroes rose in revival campaigns suggested an unhealthy influence on bondmen; and the idea of Sunday Schools, in which blacks might be taught to read the Bible, was potentially subversive.

An answer to these objections was given in 1809 by Rev. John Holt Rice, a Presbyterian minister and slave owner with a special interest in missions to the blacks:

> several persons were not at all pleased that so much notice should be taken of the negroes. To do away with all evil impressions, I took occasion to show the effect which genuine religion would have upon our servants, particularly that it would make them sober, industrious, honest, and faithful. This had the desired effect. . . .

It did not have a desired effect on Dr. Rice's black followers. With candor he reported that his argument "gave great offense to many negroes" and that for some time they boycotted his services!

Methodist and Baptist evangelists, with their appeal to raw emotion rather than intellect, appeared to have few such problems—and besides, planters found that Dr. Rice was right. Converted slaves *were* more faithful, honest, and industrious. As an enthusiastic cleric testified, planters were discovering "that their slaves are of increasing value to them when they become religious." As a result, Baptist and Methodist groups were frequently requested to send black "exhorters" to plantations, although the owners might be Episcopalians or Presbyterians. Thus, meeting houses were set up on great plantations and smaller planters made sure their slaves attended church with them—on a segregated basis, of course. Free Negroes were active in establishing their own churches and in encouraging the development of their own ministry.

It appeared, however, that some "exhorters" hid a social message within the religious message: freedom, by which they signified not only freedom from sin but also freedom from slavery. Planters, made increasingly suspicious of independent black activity by the rise of abolitionist agitation in the North, felt they were confronted with a veritable Aesopian language in Negro spirituals and sermons. When slaves sang "Steal Away to Jesus" were they looking to the hereafter or to the Underground Railroad? When preachers pictured the joys of the Promised Land were they talking about Paradise or Canada?

The worst fears of the planters seemed to be realized by the Denmark Vesey slave rebellion of 1822, involving black Methodists, and the more famous insurrection of 1831, led by Nat Turner, a Baptist "exhorter." State after state then prohibited Negro preaching without white supervision, required that Negro preachers be licensed, strictly regulated travel of free Negroes, and banned the teaching of reading and writing to blacks—a blow at the Sunday Schools. White clergymen, usually outspoken in defense of religious liberty, not only acquiesced in these restrictions but also helped enforce them. With the separation of Northern and Southern Methodists and Baptists over the issue of slavery in the early 1840's, planters felt they had little to fear in such religious instruction as might reach the slaves. The union of white plantation and white pulpit was sealed; the black church became "invisible."

With the Civil War and Reconstruction the spirit of the "invisible" church was made flesh. As Union armies penetrated into the South, Northern white missionaries, principally Methodists, Baptists, and Presbyterians, swarmed into the liberated areas. Beside them went men from the African Methodist Episcopal Church, founded in 1816; the African Methodist Episcopal Zion Church, founded in 1821; and the Western Colored Baptist Convention, established in 1853. All these represented Negro response to Northern white rejection of the concept that in the body of Christ all men were one. White and black missionaries worked arduously and successfully to stake out their claims. Under slavery only a minority of blacks had been church members; now "conversions" ran into the tens of thousands. Eventually few Negro communities, however small, failed to support at least one church. By the end of Reconstruction, 10,000 local Negro churches were estimated in operation.

The rapid growth of the visible Negro church may be attributed in large part to the fact that it served much more than a purely formal religious function. Like the parish church of the Middle Ages, the local church symbolized a community. In the words of A. A. Taylor, the Negro historian, it was the "social center . . . , the theater, the forum, and the general meeting house of the Negro community. . . . To the church all Negroes ambitious for independent leadership had to look, inasmuch as other institutions touching the life of the Negro were controlled or directed by whites." It was, as DuBois pointed out, "the first social institution fully controlled by black men in America." As such, in some places, as in the Sea Islands of South Carolina, it gradually assumed a governmental role. Unobtrusively, church elders developed their own "laws," practical rules for the governance of the community and for the settlement of disputes among church members without resort to white courts or other institutions.

Whites, Northern and Southern, viewed the emergence of independent black churches with some misgiving.

Northerners were almost universally dismayed by the unrestrained emotionalism of Negro worship. Even so loyal a friend of the black as Laura Towne, the selfless teacher of Sea Island Negroes, thought it "savage." Apparently neither she nor her white associates had visited a white frontier camp meeting. Both groups, blacks and poorer whites, were in fact responding to a common set of circumstances growing out of poverty. In orgiastic religion they found the drama and excitement otherwise lacking in their grim and monotonous lives, as well as temporary release from the tensions of everyday living. In some measure, also, these religious exercises so displeasing to genteel Yankees or English visitors, represented an assertion by the poor of their own worth, of their own values, in a society whose values were steadily being identified with the gospel of wealth.

Northerners were also troubled by the gap between religion and morality which they found among Negroes: pious blacks, for example, were not above a little fraud nor averse to amorous dalliance. Yet such behavior was not limited to blacks. Mrs. Trollope provided several interesting accounts of fraud and lechery among Northern white clerics. In the days of Reconstruction financial scandals touched the Northern Methodist publishing house and the Augustinian Fathers of Lawrence, Mass. The Baptist Home Missionary Society saw no ethical problem involved in obtaining land grant pledges from transcontinental railroads; nor did Methodists, in accepting the largesse of Daniel Drew and Cornelius Vanderbilt. In this light, it appears that Negro and white behavior, as opposed to their preachments, were much alike.

Some Yankee missionaries, especially during the war years, sought to cope with the problem by drawing the blacks into genteel churches, such as Congregational, Unitarian, or Episcopalian. The blacks, however, made it plain they preferred their own. In those places where whites and Negroes did worship together, the blacks soon asserted their right to a voice in church affairs; sometimes, in view of their numbers, a dominant voice. They even made decisions without first consulting the missionaries! No doubt this contributed to the disenchantment of some white idealists who had gone South to "do good" in a spirit of religious paternalism and found in this expression of Negro independence "ingratitude."

A major element in Southern white distrust of independent Negro congregations was fear of loss of social control over the freedmen. Still tormented by dread of insurrections (which never came), and resolutely opposed to any move which smacked of equality, native whites viewed with suspicion anything which brought Negroes together without white supervision.

At first, whites sought to resolve the problem by retaining the freedmen in established white churches, providing the Negroes were willing to accept segregation and exclusion from management of church affairs. When this failed, such churches as the Southern Methodist and Southern Presbyterian encouraged organization of separate black congregations, subject to control by white denominational bodies. This proved a failure, too. By 1866, the Negro membership in the Southern Methodist Church had dropped to 78,000, compared to 207,000 in 1860. Presbyterians reported their black membership dropped by 70 per cent.

The Southern Methodists eventually sponsored formation of a new Negro church, the Colored Methodist, which, while it won derision from many blacks as "the Old Slavery Church," did have support of whites and gradually built up a following among Negroes who did not resent such support.

To the native white, perhaps more dreaded than the loss of control over blacks, was the prospect of control passing into the hands of Northern missionaries, many of whom drew no color line, sympathized with Negro aspirations for equality, and made no attempt to disguise their distaste for the traditional Southern way of life. As early as 1866 this fear was reflected in the comment of a Virginia editor that the Northern churches operating in the South were "far more . . . political organizations than . . . religious fraternities, and, being such, are already much too strong for the public safety."

Most aggressive were the Northern Methodists. They made a strong appeal to black people with their record of abolitionism, appointment of black preachers, strong support for the Union during the war, and bitter antagonism to Andrew Johnson and all his works. In those areas of concentrated Negro population they strengthened their appeal by preaching and practicing racial equality. In 1871, for example, the South Carolina Methodist conference declared its "solemn conviction that the true basis of organization in State or Church is without distinction of *race* or *color*." Bishop Gilbert Haven publicly extolled as "the coming race in all its virile perfection" the brown men and women of Charleston, results of black and white unions. "It is an improved breed," he said, "the best the country has today." Others ardently espoused the black demand for land, even if that meant confiscation. Justice, said one missionary, demanded that "property in the South should change hands, and a just God will see to it that those who have been robbed of their earnings for generations shall not fail to obtain their share. . . . In the golden age coming, the planters of the South will be black men."

Such appeals were reinforced by Methodist "good works" in aid to freedmen, such as the building of Negro schools, colleges, and medical schools; by encouraging the development of Negro preachers; and by the Methodist emphasis on revivalist religion. By 1869, the Methodist Episcopal Church, North, which had no following at all in 1860, had ten annual conferences functioning in the South, two-thirds of whose membership were black. By the 1890's, the church had enrolled 254,000 Negro members, as compared to 73,000 whites.

But Northern Methodism had a flaw—it was basically a white church. This provided an opening for black Methodist groups, which, so far as popular appeal was concerned, more than compensated for lack of financial resources and other internal weaknesses. In addition, black Methodists were much less active than Northern Methodists in promoting social Reconstruction. Thus, they encountered less of the native white antagonism which so often met the efforts of the Northern Methodists. This made black missionary work easier, and it also provided a field for work among those Negroes who had little desire to come into conflict with white society. In ten years, 1860–1870, the African Methodist Episcopal Zion Church grew from 27,000 members to 200,000. The African Methodist Episcopal Church, which prior to the war had no Southern following, by 1880 had 400,000 members, most of whom were Southern blacks.

Methodism, in one form or another, was successful in reaching the freedmen—but its success was much less than that of the Baptists. Paradoxically, this was largely because the Baptists were not as well organized as the Methodists. The Methodists had a developed church structure, a well-organized system of church government, and a large measure of control over local preachers and congregations. This was true also of other groups which conducted missionary enterprises among Negroes—Presbyterians, Episcopalians, Congregationalists. It was not true of Baptists. In that denomination each local church literally governed itself, with no accounting to superior bodies. Each church chose its own preacher, set its own code of discipline, and financed itself. Members were even free to secede and establish another church. Such voluntarism, with its prospect of allowing one to participate actively in a truly self-governing independent society, appealed strongly to men and women who had never been allowed to make a major decision of their own. Here at last was an institution that made black freedom meaningful; here was a black institution in which black people were free to make their own mistakes.

There were other reasons for the phenomenal growth of Negro Baptist churches. Capable and ambitious but untrained men found opportunities for leadership in a church which placed greater emphasis on character and personality than on formal education. An energetic individual might serve as preacher of one church and at the same time found numerous other churches in his locality. Many freedmen, accustomed to Baptist "exhorters" on the plantations or to attending Baptist churches with their masters, naturally gravitated in freedom toward the new black Baptist congregations. In addition, many free Southern Negroes had been Baptists, and added their persuasion to that of the Northern black Baptist missionaries who came into the South during and after the war. And in the local church, common black men and women could give expression to their profoundest feelings without a patronizing white observing and calling it "savage." It is not surprising that in many areas the Baptists outstripped all other denominations in terms of membership and in some actually outnumbered all others together.

But this triumph of religious particularism, however satisfying it may have been to those involved, had within it potential dangers to the Negro community as a whole. Native whites, while tolerating the development of Negro institutions free of white control, were by no means reconciled to them, as the murder of outspoken black preachers demonstrated. In this context, if the Negro community were to make its way toward equality, it required, not separatism, but cohesiveness and discipline. But most freedmen, including many of their leaders, were hardly aware of the problem.

Eager to test themselves in freedom, Negroes tended to make their churches centers of self-expression to the utmost. Minor disagreements in a congregation tended to become reasons for separation; separation led to new local churches. Thus, there was a proliferation of local churches, most of them, especially in the rural areas, weak and poor. Lacking adequate funds, they paid their ministers little or nothing. The ministers, then, earned their livelihood in secular occupations, which meant in many instances that the ministers depended for their daily bread on white goodwill. While from their ranks came some capable men, they were as poor and untutored as the people they led.

Some church leaders saw the dangers implicit in such a situation, either from purely denominational considerations or from a larger social understanding. Methodists strove to bring some measure of order through their conferences; Baptists worked to organize district and state associations to provide guidance to local churches and to consolidate their influence. Such efforts were only partially successful.

Both the strength and the weaknesses of the Negro church made it an object of white attention in the years after Reconstruction. Here was an all-Negro institution enjoying the uncritical loyalty of the black masses on the one hand, but, on the other, suffering from division, often abjectly poor, and lacking a social philosophy which would at once unify the blacks and articulate their aspirations. Operating on the same principle that colonial powers had found so useful, native whites perceived that shrewd employment of a black institution would facilitate reassertion of white supremacy. So, making full use of economic and political power, whites rewarded those ministers who dutifully accepted a submissive role and punished those who did not. The punishment need not be obtrusive: the simple withdrawal of white goodwill was sufficient. If the offending preacher did not get the message, his followers did; if he still persisted in error, he was soon looking for a new pulpit. In this way, "troublemakers" were weeded out, thanks also in part to Negro informers, who, for reasons of their own, sought to curry favor with whites. Ironically, the one social institution which Negroes could call their own became a prime instrument through which they were conditioned to responses appropriate to a white racist society.

Nevertheless, despite its failings, the Negro church contributed no little to the active role of the Negro during Reconstruction. From the ranks of its preachers came many notable leaders of the period, for, as Sir George Campbell observed, they were preachers because they were leaders, rather than leaders because they were preachers. Richard H. Cain, Congressman from South Carolina and a political power in the state, first came to public notice as the popular African Methodist preacher in Charleston. Hiram R. Revels, the Mississippi senator, was an ordained minister of the same church. Benjamin F. Randolph, who was rapidly becoming a significant Negro spokesman in South Carolina until his assassination in 1868, was a Northern Methodist missionary. Among other outstanding men who came from the ranks of the church were J. Sella Martin, editor of the official organ of the Negro National Labor Union; Jonathan C. Gibbs, Secretary of State and later Superintendent of Education in Florida; and James W. Hood, who helped organize the public school system of North Carolina.

If the church provided opportunities for black leadership to emerge, it no less afforded countless members of the rank-and-file training in the management of everyday affairs—"a very important education," as

Sir George Campbell noted. In the operation of their numerous local churches black men and women, often for the first time in their lives, were the decision-makers. In developing the means by which to make wise decisions they learned how to cope with problems of finances, planning, cooperation, and management. The lessons thus learned stood them in good stead in business and social life. In short, within the limits set by white society, Negroes learned some of the skills and arts of self-government through the church.

Perhaps the church's greatest contribution, however, was its *being*. Its very existence helped to maintain a sense of Negro identity and community and to nourish an indigenous black culture. If, in the Reconstruction years, the church gave black men their first opportunity to handle their own affairs in their own institution, in the ensuing years it helped shelter the black community against white hostility, manifested not only in lynchings, race riots, and segregation, but also in the open advocacy of genocide. The price paid by the church, as by school and college, was high: accommodation to white supremacy. But if the issue were black survival, who can say the price was too high?

CHAPTER **4**

Not-So-Black
Reconstruction

So far we have examined national Reconstruction policy and noted how the black man fared under it, economically, educationally, spiritually. How did he function as citizen? Here the answer must be limited to the Southern states, for only there were black men present in sufficient number to make their votes count, and outside of the South few black men attained public office. Even in the South black political power was never dominant—it was effectively circumscribed by white power, whether exercised by friends or foes. Given the fluid nature of Southern Reconstruction politics, it happened not infrequently that the black man found yesterday's white friend today's opponent and an erstwhile enemy professing devotion to black cooperation. This was in a sense recognition of black power; it was also realization of that power's limits and weaknesses. It was important enough to be courted, but not so unified and organized that it could not be challenged, as we shall see in the following chapter. If we are to understand the political role of the black man, therefore, we must first look at the white influences which helped shape and limit that role.

These influences may be conveniently divided into two major categories: friendly and hostile. The former were largely those whites, Yankee and Southern, who worked with black men in the Republican party. The latter, mostly native whites, called themselves variously Democrats, Conservative-Democrats, or simply Conservatives. We shall use the term Conservative to include all such groupings.

White Republicans included men whose concern for the Negro

ranged all the way from disinterested idealism to unscrupulous pursuit of personal gain.

Among the Northerners were those who stayed on in the South after the war because they felt a moral obligation to the freedmen. Such were Laura Towne, who persisted in her educational work in South Carolina long after Reconstruction, and General Samuel C. Armstrong, under whose guidance Hampton Institute became a major force in Negro education.

There were also those who came to do good and remained to do well, such as Reuben Tomlinson, the Pennsylvania bank clerk who had been a member of the pioneer group in the Sea Islands. After the war he entered politics and business, actively promoting railroad and ferti-lizer enterprises in his adopted state. A powerful force in the promotion of Negro education, he was an active ally of black Republicans until 1872, when, victim of a Conservative campaign to split the Republicans, he lost many of his black supporters.

Other allies included Northern missionaries—Methodist, Baptist, Presbyterian. While some confined their evangelism to traditional salvationist appeals, others felt the religious message irrelevant with-out ethical application to the problems of the black man. This con-cern, as well as a feeling that church membership was meaningless without education, found expression in the founding of Negro schools and colleges. It also found expression in a virtual political alliance with Republicans. "They preach their religion and their politics at the same time," grumbled a native white Alabamian. One wonders whether he objected equally to the anti-Reconstruction politics preached from many native white pulpits at the time.

Northerners turned Southern politicians also cultivated black power. Some, like Adelbert Ames, Maine Yankee, later governor of Mississippi, sought in principle to root the Republican party in the South as a biracial organization. Some, such as Henry Clay Warmoth of Illinois, who became governor of Louisiana, cynically exploited black votes and aspirations to promote their own fortunes.

Southern Republicans were almost as diverse as Northerners in their attitudes toward black political power. A few had been Democrats who resigned themselves to Reconstruction and decided that working through the Republican party was the best means of maintaining white in-fluence. James L. Orr, long prominent in South Carolina politics, was typical of this group. Many of the leaders had been old-line Southern Whigs, who found in the Republican outlook a congenial, updated version of their old faith in the Union, social stability, and the rights of property. Also, they argued, since Republican rule was inevitable, it afforded the safest way in which black men could be tutored in the ways of citizenship. Besides, through the Republican party they hoped to manipulate the black vote in the interest of planters and urban businessmen against the crudely class-conscious poorer whites, traditionally hostile to Whiggery. Their outlook was symbolized by James L. Alcorn of Mississippi, great planter and Confederate general, who asserted that only collaboration between white men and black could save the state from "inevitable ruin."

A similar conclusion, reached from entirely different premises, led many poorer whites into the Republican ranks. Like S. G. W. Dill of South Carolina, they believed that through alliance with black men they could change the laws of debt and contract which bore heavily on the poor, obtain more equitable tax laws, and through free public education open up new opportunities for their children.

Other Southern Republicans had less lofty motives. Promoters, such as George W. Swepson of North Carolina, utilized black politicians as well as white to obtain governmental favor in carrying out their fraudulent schemes. Governor Franklin J. Moses of South Carolina was as cynical as Warmoth of Louisiana in exploiting black power, but so adroit was he in catering to black feeling that honest black leaders, such as Francis L. Cardozo, Secretary of State and later State Treasurer, found it almost impossible to undermine his influence.

The black-white alliance within the Republican party was at best an uneasy one. Apart from a handful of Yankee idealists, most white Republicans believed in white supremacy—not as blatantly as white Conservatives, but certainly as deeply. Occupying key party positions, they treated black men as junior partners in the coalition, even in such states as South Carolina, Mississippi and Louisiana, where the black vote was of major significance. The number of black men in major public office was held to a minimum. In the distribution of minor offices a disproportionately small share went to blacks. Whites cultivated black power when business promotions were at stake, but in matters of public policy they tempered their zeal for black support with consideration for native white prejudice. Thus, in states such as Louisiana, where segregated schools were presumably outlawed, integrated schools were rare. Civil rights laws were passed in many states, but as in South Carolina, they were rarely enforced.

At first, blacks had little choice but to accept junior status. Negro voters were as yet poorly organized and their leaders new to the ways of politics. Some, typified by Beverly Nash of South Carolina, doubted their abilities, and many were fearful of arousing too much white antagonism. As experience provided knowledge and confidence, the black attitude changed: junior status was no longer acceptable. Negroes pressed for increased recognition in party councils and in the allocation of public offices and for implementation of public policy relative to black needs. At this point—but not for this reason alone— the Republican coalition began to come apart.

By 1872 some white leaders—exemplified by Orr in South Carolina and Warmoth in Louisiana—were in revolt against the regular party organizations. While they drew some Negro leaders into their campaigns, their subtle racist appeals as well as hope of splitting the Republican party brought them Conservative support. In 1873, when Alcorn tried to capture control of Mississippi, he frankly bid for Conservative support by making the issue that of saving the state from "black domination."

Thus, even in the party of his "friends," the role of the black man was circumscribed. Most white Republicans, Yankee and Southern alike, promoted black power because they had no alternative—without it they could not retain power. This meant concessions had to be made to black interests, but whites tried to confine the concessions to the minimum necessary to keep black votes in line without at the same time alienating further that native white sentiment which they hoped to win over. Beyond that they were willing to go only as far as black pressure compelled them—and the influence of that pressure was diluted by the fact that when strongly applied it divided and weakened the only party on which black hopes rested.

Black political power, then, was limited even within the Republican party. It was further limited by the active opposition of the Conservatives—an opposition the more effective because it embraced within it the mass of native whites who rejected Reconstruction and especially resented the new independent role of the black man.

Since, by shattering effective use of black political power to advance black causes, Conservatism played a key role in overthrowing Reconstruction governments and set the conditions under which black people were to live for a generation after Reconstruction, it is essential that we study the movement in some detail.

Unlike Republicans, who had relatively little success in converting native whites, Conservatives operated from a wide power base among their own people. Their influence extended all the way from the great planters and businessmen who wooed the black man the better to control him through the middle reaches of society to the mass of poorer whites who wanted no truck with black men at all.

Their very diversity was a source of strength, for it traversed the spectrum of Southern white life. Possessed of a Robert E. Lee, who enjoyed universal respect, they also had a Nathan B. Forrest, former slave trader and Confederate general, who gathered scattered Klan organizations into a unified Invisible Empire. Wade Hampton, the South Carolina aristocrat who courted the Negro vote, was a Conservative—as was Hinton R. Helper, the erstwhile native white critic of slavery, who now looked forward to black extinction, either through "natural decay" or genocide. Robert Toombs of Georgia thought that through Conservatism he could restore the era of plantation and mint julep. Others, such as John C. Brown of Tennessee and John B. Gordon of Georgia, cut from the same cloth as the Northern "robber barons," more successfully used Conservatism to set the South on the road of business and industrial development.

Furnishing the sinews through which such leaders could wage their war against Reconstruction were the masses of obscure whites—farmers, mechanics, merchants—hostile to black aspirations. These supplied political muscle through legal political organizations. They also constituted the manpower for the myriad secret societies which employed terrorism to curb black aspirations.

Conservatism, however, was not a unified whole—there were too many deep divisions between poor whites and aristocrats, farmers and business men, laborers and employers, to permit that. But one overriding dogma bound them together: white supremacy. This furnished Conservatives an emotion-laden, clear-cut objective—a "gut" issue transcending all others.

Indeed, within the framework of white supremacy there was the prospect of accommodating rival native white interests. Craftsmen, and unskilled workers in the booming cotton textile industry, would be protected from black competition. Such workers would be thus more willing to accommodate themselves to their employers—it is significant that the great strike wave of 1877 touched the South hardly at all. Exclusion of black labor from the better-paying occupations would render it also more docile, and so restore to the countryside the orderly racial relationship in which black men served in subordination.

The "new men" saw in white supremacy a road to political power which would assure *their* rule in the new South of business and industry they were fostering and also provide them significant leverage in dealing with Northern capital coming South. To the poorest whites, white supremacy meant that once again they would have a people to look down on, and so compensate for the general contempt in which they were held by white society.

But Conservatism was more than the sum of its parts, more basic than a grand accommodation of Southern interests. In a profound psychological sense the call for white supremacy represented a native white response to the traumatic experience of utter defeat in war, and in particular to the emergence of the black man as free citizen in consequence of that defeat. Under Reconstruction, indeed, the black man seemed to be on the way to power: he voted, held public office, sat on juries, testified in court against white men, dominated the armed state militias. Whites, as well as blacks, were ready to believe, as a popular Negro song of the day had it, that the "bottom rail" was on top.

The belief was ill-founded. In an era when economic overshadowed political power, Negroes were far from being the top rail. They owned no coal fields, no iron mines, no railroad systems, no cotton mills. They owned some land, but relatively little in comparison with white holdings. As we noted earlier, the mass of them were miserably poor. Nor, as we shall see, did they exercise control of any state government; such political power as they had was limited. But the song had an element of truth in it: bottom rail had not become top rail, but it *had* moved up— and being a black rail among white, it was highly visible.

To native whites this appeared revolutionary, an overturning of the eternal verities of race relationships. Apart from Southerners who had gone over to the Republicans, most agreed with Howell Cobb, the Georgian planter and Confederate general, that slavery "provided the best system of labor that could be devised for the negro race"; that abolition had been "unfortunate" in its results; and that the task of statesmanship was to "provide a substitute" for slavery. This was written in 1865, but the idea pervaded white thought long after, and was given new point by the rise of the bottom rail under Reconstruction.

The ability of the bottom rail to rise has always been assumed to be a particular virtue of American society, but in this case, it was held, the rule did not apply. *This* rail, being black, was *by nature* inferior, and thus incapable of much improvement. Historical, biblical, and scientific authority agreed on this point. To allow blacks into positions of power, therefore, was to place a superior at the mercy of an inferior race. Thus, the very foundations of good government were threatened.

More, Anglo-Saxon civilization, presumed to be the best of its kind, was endangered. The upward surge of the black man posed the ultimate danger: the mixing of "human and brute blood," as one planter put it in another connection. To many native whites this was not a remote but an immediate menace.

In some states, Reconstruction governments, in getting rid of the discriminatory legislation bequeathed them by Johnson governments, had removed the bans against interracial marriage. Such marriages did take place. More often they were between white men and black women, but in some instances white women married black men. That white men should possess black women was tolerable, although increasingly in disfavor during Reconstruction. That black men should take white women as wives was abhorrent. It flew in the face of that cult of pure white womanhood through which the pre-war South had regulated its sexual behavior, and it fed the fears of white masculinity already nourished by the myths of Negro male sexuality.

It was thus easy for whites to believe that the dire prediction of John C. Calhoun was coming true. Once emancipation came, he had warned, "the next step would be to raise the negroes to a social and political equality with the whites; and that being effected, we would soon find the present condition of the two races reversed. They, and their northern allies would be the masters, and we the slaves; . . ."

To distraught whites, Conservatism offered a way out from such catastrophe. Cultivating the myth of the Lost Cause, it sanctified the past; since no sin had been committed, no repentance was necessary. For the future it held out the hope of white supremacy restored under the leadership of Southern men, many of them heroes of the holy war for Southern independence. For the present, it afforded opportunity for action through legitimate political activity to subvert and eventually overthrow the Reconstruction governments and the black power associated with them. More immediately, through the numerous secret societies, of which the Ku Klux Klan was the most notorious, black power could be curbed by intimidation and violence. In these ways Conservatism served to restore the native white psychological wholeness so badly disrupted by defeat in war. And it was the black man who had to pay the bill—even before Reconstruction ended.

So much, then, for the white forces which restricted the black man's functioning as a first-class citizen. How did he behave, what did he think, under such conditions?

Of basic importance, although all too little studied in light of contemporary knowledge of psychology, is the fact that in the course of a few years black Americans underwent two experiential shocks, perhaps even more profound than the trauma of military defeat for native whites. First was the sudden change from the relatively orderly paternalism of slavery to a chaotic, impersonal freedom in an embittered and war-ravaged land. The second shock was that, contrary to all black expectations and understandings, they were denied free land. Better than

Frederick Douglass, who uttered the words, they perceived that freedom under such circumstances meant turning them over "naked to their enemies." To protect their new freedom, and to give it meaning, black men turned to the means made available to them through the Reconstruction acts and the Fourteenth and Fifteenth Amendments—politics. In the context of Southern politics, that meant Republican politics.

As we have seen, few white Republicans were willing to accept them as equals. Such an eventuality apparently escaped the imaginations of Northern friends of the Negro. The American Anti-Slavery Society, for instance, solemnly assured black men that adoption of the Fifteenth Amendment "secured to them equal political rights with the white race, or, if any single right be still doubtful, places them in such circumstances that they can easily achieve it." This placed black men in a dilemma. On the one hand they were assured by Northerners that they enjoyed full legal and political equality. On the other hand, when they pressed for it within their own party they were rebuffed or advised not to push too much too fast. Or, if they sought to apply the principle in Southern situations they were often met with violence—a violence the more widespread because it was rarely punished.

In a larger sense the black man in Reconstruction was confronted with the problem of identity which had vexed free Negroes like David Walker since long before the war. Was the Negro a black man or an American? Could he be both? During Reconstruction black men strove to prove they could be both. Or, perhaps more accurately, to use the words of DuBois in another connection, the black sought to "attain self-conscious manhood" by merging "his double self into a truer and better self," which combined the best elements of Americanism and *négritude*.

Unfortunately, the black man during Reconstruction was in no position to take the initiative. Psychologically, he was at a disadvantage in that as a free man in an individualistic, competitive society he had to cope with a host of problems for which slavery had been but poor preparation. Numerically, he was handicapped in that in most states he constituted only a minority of the population. By and large he had little education, which meant he was often bewildered in the white man's world of law and contract, to say nothing of the feelings of inadequacy to which such ignorance gave rise. No black men occupied the heights of industry and finance, nor enjoyed the political influence which such possession entailed. The political heights were more accessible, but even there, as we have noted, the summits remained safely in white hands.

Public opinion in the South was almost entirely hostile to black aspirations, while in the North support for the black man was diminishing.

One after another of the secular abolitionist and freedmen's aid societies folded their tents, satisfied that a good work had been well done. Given equality in law and equality of opportunity, the black man was now free to prove himself.

Although black men possessed no means of taking the initiative, it is unwise to conclude then that they were merely pawns in a white power struggle. They might lack education and property, but they did have votes—and those votes were important. Indeed, in some areas of the South they were decisive. White politicians, Republicans and Conservative, sought to cultivate, control, or, in the case of some Conservatives, neutralize, those votes. This meant that Negroes had bargaining power. They might not be able to get land for black men, but they could and did force concessions on other matters of importance to them: education, civil rights, social reform, and economic development, with its promise of eventual release from rural poverty. Since concessions were forthcoming more readily and more extensively from Republicans, and since Negroes realized that behind Conservative promises lay determination to keep the South a white man's country, most black men naturally voted Republican.

Further, the Negroes produced their own leadership, which enabled them to make good use of what bargaining power they had. This point needs some emphasis, for deeply implanted in the mythology of this period is the notion that black men did not, indeed could not, develop significant leaders. Some disappeared so completely from the historical record that they are not mentioned in the *Dictionary of American Biography*. In fact, a listing of the black men who contributed substantially to American life during Reconstruction would take us far beyond the scope of this work. Let it suffice to mention a few of the more outstanding:

U.S. Senators Hiram R. Revels and Blanche K. Bruce of Mississippi; and Congressmen Richard H. Cain of South Carolina, James T. Rapier of Alabama, and John R. Lynch of Mississippi—all of whom played active roles in both national and state politics;

Francis L. Cardozo, the able and honest State Treasurer of South Carolina;

Prince Rivers, former coachman and Civil War veteran, who helped write the South Carolina constitution, served several years in the legislature, and became a Major-General in the state militia;

Isaac Myers, ship caulker from Baltimore, who strove to unite white and black labor into integrated unions;

Paul Trevigne, son of a veteran of the War of 1812, who, as editor of the New Orleans *Tribune,* served to articulate the aspirations of the Louisiana freedmen;

Richard T. Greener, professor at the University of South Carolina, who helped to organize the public school system of the state and played a leading part in Republican politics although never elected to public office.

Where did this leadership come from? Some were Southern free Negroes who had been artisans, farmers, preachers, teachers. Others came from the North, often possessed of educational qualifications surpassing those of their white contemporaries. Still others were descendants of Underground Railroad travelers who had escaped to Canada. Some were Union Army veterans, who had demonstrated capacity for leadership as non-commissioned officers. Many were former slaves, whose talents gave testimony to the latent creative energies long suppressed in an enslaved people. Among these former slaves were Senator Bruce of Mississippi, and Congressmen J. H. Rainey of South Carolina, and John R. Lynch of Mississippi.

No doubt black bargaining power would have been greater had Negroes constituted a compact, disciplined political group. This was indeed what the Loyal Leagues had in mind when they set about to develop a Republican political consciousness among the blacks—but their success was much less than their Conservative opponents claimed. Negroes were no more a monolithic unit than were Southern or Northern whites.

Socially, they were divided according to pre-war status. Free Negroes tended to draw a line between themselves and former slaves, and within the ranks of "old free" blacks there were gradations according to lightness of skin, with those who claimed blood relationship to prominent white families looking upon themselves as an "elite." Even before the war this "social distance" manifested itself, as when the Brown Fellowship Society, made up of light-skinned shopkeepers and artisans of Charleston, barred blacks from membership. These retorted by organizing the Free Dark Men of Color. Generally, in terms of Negro society, the advantage lay with the light skinned, for they often had received good education, and in terms of the Negro community, were wealthy. (Both were attributable, in part, to the benevolence of white ancestors.)

Thus, when Reconstruction opened the gates of opportunity, they poured through, assuming many posts of leadership. This, in turn, posed problems, for the elite was primarily interested in political issues and civil rights, while the masses were concerned with economic rights, especially ownership of land. That such differences within the black community did not become a source of discord, as they did in some islands of the Caribbean, was due largely to native whites. To them, a light-skinned Negro, as well as a dark, was still a "nigger," the more to be "kept in his place" because of the belief that the infusion of white blood made the light-skinned Negro more intelligent, and therefore more dangerous. When the chips were down, the elite Negro had no place to go except with his black brethren.

There were also political divisions within the Negro community. Then, as now, there was a considerable number of blacks, as of whites, who were apathetic. Passive people, playing no positive historic role, are apt to be passed over in history books, but in a given situation, as in Reconstruction, they do play a role: by their inertia they act as a drag on the progress of their people as a whole. More, during Reconstruction, they were susceptible to appeals like that of Sydenham Porter of Alabama, who counselled his fellow-blacks to ignore politics, "go to work, and cherish good and kind feelings toward our old friends [the planters]."

There were some Negroes who for various reasons chose to follow the Conservative line, even though that meant weakening the bargaining power of the black people as a whole. Their rationale was set forth by a group of Alabama Negro Democrats in 1872. Starting from the premise that the interests of Southern whites and blacks were "one and in common," they argued that prosperity of Southern blacks depended on friendly relations with whites, and that native whites were now committed to protect black rights, evidenced by Conservative acceptance of the Liberal Republican candidates, Horace Greeley and Gratz Brown, as their own.

Even among Negro Republicans there was division. One division was along class lines. For example, Francis L. Cardozo, a well-to-do free Negro from Charleston, argued in the South Carolina constitutional convention against a provision permitting a moratorium on debt collection, a measure that had strong support among whites hard-pressed to meet their obligations after the war's destruction, and also among many blacks. In some states proposals, supported by black men, for raising wage standards were opposed not only by white planters but also by black leaders.

Black Republicans were also split by the factional struggles within the party, usually reflecting quarrels between rival white economic interests over such issues as state aid to railroads. Except in Mississippi, where such aid was prohibited by the state constitution, there was no

dispute as to states granting aid—the question was which of the contending groups was to benefit. As the process developed, and as corruption became more evident, the party also divided between regulars and
reformers—and again Negro ranks were divided.

Thus, while the mass of blacks tended to be Regular Republicans,
they were not a united body. This meant that their bargaining power
was limited. Yet limited though it was, its influence was felt in the
course of Reconstruction history.

Its influence was felt, but it did not dominate. This was the extent
of "black power," the limit of "black Reconstruction." In no Southern
state did black men ever control the machinery of government. In South
Carolina, where blacks were most potent in terms of population and
leadership, they constituted a majority only in the lower house of the
legislature—never in the Senate. Nor did they ever control the executive or judicial branches. In other states—including Mississippi, with
its preponderant black population—their direct political influence was
even less. In county and municipal posts Negroes were only a minority
of office-holders; most were held by native and Northern whites.

It should be noted, however, that sometimes the offices to which blacks
were appointed were of key importance to the ordinary black farmer or
laborer. Joel Williamson, in his study of the South Carolina Negro
during Reconstruction, has reported that many blacks were appointed to
the low judicial office of Trial Justice[1]—but this was precisely the office
which passed on small claims, involving one hundred dollars or less.
Such cases often involved white planters and black laborers, tenants,
and sharecroppers. These courts, then, represented the closest contact of
the ordinary black man with government. To him, it was significant of
the new order of things that his claim received fair, even sympathetic,
consideration. By the same token, planters felt aggrieved that their
claims were not taken at face value.

It used to be argued that black power was to be construed not only
in terms of direct political participation but also in view of a backup
military force which sustained it. That is, the South was supposedly
occupied by hordes of federal troops who supported black political and
social aspirations. The fact is that the federal army was demobilized
at an incredible rate after Appomattox. When the war ended, more than
a million officers and men were enrolled. Within a year this had shrunk
to 57,000, and by 1876 to 28,565. The mass of the troops was deployed
in the West, manning frontier forts, and waging almost incessant cam-

[1] Joel Williamson, *op. cit.*, p. 114.

paigns against Indian peoples—Apaches, Sioux, Cheyennes, Comanches. Those stationed in the South were spread thin: in 1874 President Grant reported 4,082 federal soldiers on duty throughout the entire region (excluding Texas, a center of war against Indians). Great areas of the South never saw a federal soldier after the war; in others, troops were withdrawn as soon as stable governments were established.

Nor were the attitudes of the troops especially friendly toward black men. By the end of 1866 all black troops had been removed from the South, following Grant's recommendation that such transfer be made for "obvious reasons." Enlisted men and officers tended to identify themselves with Southern whites and Southern white interests. Indeed, while Andrew Johnson was in office (and that was until March 4, 1869) officers who did not please native whites were apt to find themselves replaced, as were John Pope in Georgia and Edward Ord in Mississippi.

An extreme but suggestive example of how far some army commanders were willing to go in collaborating with native whites is that of General Alvin C. Gillem, who succeeded Ord in Mississippi. Before the state was readmitted in 1870, Gillem made a deal with Edmund Richardson, a wealthy planter and speculator, whereby the state's convicts—most of whom were black—were turned over to him to work on his plantations, while the state paid him $30,000 a year for maintenance and transportation! It is small wonder that when Gillem was later transferred to Texas, it was "to the general regret of the conservative whites."

There was, of course, a way in which black power was manifested indirectly through white spokesmen and representatives. Just as white workers, in the early stages of union organization, lacking adequate leadership among themselves and anxious to persuade hostile public opinion, turned to middle-class lawyers, editors, and preachers, so did many blacks turn to whites. There was an active and intelligent black leadership, as we have seen, but its numbers were inadequate to serve the needs of nearly four million black people. There were also shrewd Negroes who sensed that there was real political "muscle" in backing white politicians—these were more acceptable to the white community, and because they knew where their power base lay, were able and willing to further black aspirations. And there were some who, distrustful of successful people of their own race, preferred to support white men.

Black bargaining power, then, is to be found not only in the direct expression of black leadership, but also in the white leadership which depended on black votes, such as Moses in South Carolina and Ames in Mississippi. The extent and limits of such bargaining power are to be seen in the constitutions and legislation of the Reconstruction era and in their actual application.

The limitations may be summed up in the observation that Radical Reconstruction was not very radical, in the sense that radicalism implies basic changes in economic, social, and political relations. The fact that Reconstruction was basically conservative helped to undercut the radical promise of a new day in race relationships, as we noted in the discussion of the national failure to provide land for the freedmen.

This was reflected also in fundamental political decisions. The framers of Reconstruction devised no new means through which to attain their ends. They sought merely to restore the old Constitution, in John Marshall's sense of its providing "an indissoluble union of indestructible states." This meant, in the words of Albion W. Tourgee, an active and perceptive participant in Reconstruction as a judge in North Carolina, that Southern states once more became "self-regulating and sovereign" in their domestic affairs. This opened the way for native whites to regain control. As Tourgee observed, Reconstruction legislation left these whites and blacks "like cocks in a pit" to battle for such control; it "said to the colored man, . . . , 'Root, hog, or die!'" Foreseeing the danger, Radicals like Thaddeus Stevens had proposed holding the states in federal tutelage until the rights of black men were safe. Such a revolutionary suggestion found little support among Congressmen and Senators who were anything but revolutionary!

Thus, the old federal-state structure was adhered to, and within each state the traditional separation of executive, judicial, and legislative power was followed, as was the hallowed practice of two-house legislatures. In keeping with this approach, the new constitutions were patterned on Northern models. Some granted sweeping powers to the governor, especially in the area of appointments, apparently reflecting hopes of white delegates that the office would be filled by white men who would keep black officeholders to the minimum necessary for peaceful co-existence of the races.

The essentially conservative character of Reconstruction was shown also in state action, or inaction, on key issues. Except for South Carolina, no state made any effort to provide land for the freedmen—and even there, as we have seen, the program fell far short of black needs. No state concerned itself with protecting the rights of labor. Legislative proposals to raise wage standards were defeated, and union activity frowned upon: in South Carolina the militia was used to break a farm labor strike. No state adopted the suggestion put forward by leading black legislators that women, white and black, be allowed to vote.

Neither courts nor legislature restricted property rights in any significant way: the sanctity of property and contract was still held inviolable. Indeed, the crop-lien laws passed during the Reconstruction era to assure merchants their legal due by compelling debtors to market their crops through their creditors tightened the law of contract in such a way as to fasten upon white and black farmers a system of virtual peonage.

Next to failure to meet the land problem, perhaps the worst sin of omission of the Reconstruction governments was their failure to abolish the infamous convict-leasing systems they inherited from Johnson governments and Union generals. Under this system, for a few cents a day (except in the Gillem case already noted) states and counties leased out to private contractors the services of prisoners to work in mines and turpentine camps, on levees, construction jobs, and plantations. Contractors preferred to lease blacks. The result was a new system of slavery, in which Negroes guilty of no more offense than a petty crime against property were condemned to servitude often worse than that of pre-war slavery and often to death, for the mortality rate was excessive: in the post-Reconstruction years in Mississippi black prisoners died at a rate of 11 per cent while the white rate was 5.3 per cent. The worst features of the system did not appear until the advent of the Conservatives, of course, but the fact that the Reconstruction governments did nothing to end it tells us much of the nature of those governments.

Perhaps even more striking in the Reconstruction governments' adherence to traditional constitutional concepts was their tolerance of opposition. Truly revolutionary governments would have gagged hostile preachers, silenced critical editors, driven out dissenting professors, and so manipulated public opinion as to produce at least superficial concensus—just as Southern states had done for over a generation prior to the war. Such a policy was not even considered. Not only were opponents free to speak and write—they were also free to organize politically and to elect their representatives to state office, a freedom which Conservatives exploited to the utmost.

While the fulminations of Hinton R. Helper helped stimulate white antagonism to blacks, men like Confederate General Henry A. Wise developed the mythology of the Lost Cause. In an address that was widely commented on in white newspapers, Wise declared, "The noblest band of men who ever fought or fell in the annals of war, . . . were, I exultingly claim, the private soldiers in the armies of the great Confederate cause." Benjamin H. Hill, former Confederate Senator, published a lengthy pamphlet attacking the Reconstruction laws as unconstitutional; he advised President Johnson to refuse enforcement and native whites to ignore military rule. Such utterances were mild compared to the emotion-laden appeals of editors who subtly promoted the Ku Klux Klan in their newspapers. Native white Republicans were singled out for abuse; in the words of one Georgia editor, they had "dishonored the dignity of the white blood, and are traitors alike to principle and to race."

Such freedom of dissent did not long survive the end of Reconstruction. Just as the pre-war South would permit no questioning of slavery, so the Conservative South tolerated no challenge to white supremacy. When one of its great writers, George Washington Cable, published in 1885 a sharp criticism of current Southern white treatment of the blacks, the outcry against him was so bitter that it played a significant part in his decision to move to Massachusetts. Lesser known men simply stopped speaking out—which gave point to the title of Cable's work, *The Silent South.*

The limits of black bargaining power were shown even more clearly in the Congress. Direct black influence was minimal, largely because there was not much of it: two Senators and twenty Congressmen. Not all of these served in any one session—apparently the highest number of black Congressmen at any one time was seven, of a total of 292 members. Their direct influence was also minimal: few Northerners depended on black votes. Because the blacks were newcomers they had little seniority, and thus rarely attained positions of power on committees where the actual work of Congress is done. Because they were black, they were, with a few exceptions, treated correctly but coldly by Republicans and with marked hostility by Democrats. They were quite powerless after Democrats captured control of the House of Representatives in the fourty-fourth Congress (1875) and the self-styled Redeemers took over the South in 1877.

Two major problems preoccupied black legislators: education and civil rights. Knowing that federal aid was essential to provide sound school systems for the South, they proposed federal land grants to provide funds for schools. They had sound precedents: the Northwest Ordinance of 1787, providing a section in each township for support of schools; the Morrill Land Grant Act of 1862 to establish agricultural and mechanical colleges; and, of course, the lavish grants given railroads. Their arguments fell on deaf ears, as did those of white colleagues who proposed other ways of providing federal aid to Southern schools. Negroes did win a Civil Rights Act in 1875, outlawing discrimination in transportation, theaters, restaurants, and hotels. It was poorly enforced, and the Supreme Court knocked it out eight years later. Black men had to wait 90 years for another civil rights law and a Supreme Court more sympathetic to their needs and aspirations.

The interest of black Congressmen was not confined to these problems, of course. Like white Congressmen anxious for reelection they fought to get federal funds for local improvements and to provide tariff protection for farmers and manufacturers who claimed to be hurt by foreign competition. They tried to get fairer treatment for American Indians and to establish a national board of health. They also strove to eliminate racial discrimination in the army and to procure equal pensions for Civil War veterans without regard to race.

The record of Senator Bruce of Mississippi is indicative of how a black legislator in the nation's capital fared. He succeeded in getting many of his constituents who were war veterans pensions which they had been denied. He did not succeed in getting the Treasury to set aside funds due Negroes in a special fund to aid black education, nor did his measures to control the liquor traffic make much headway—and of course the latter did not endear him to one of the most powerful lobbies in the country. He spoke out in vain against unfair federal policies in regard to American Indians and against the proposals to shut off Chinese immigration.

His efforts on behalf of the depositors of the ill-starred Freedmen's Bank resulted in his becoming chairman of the committee which wound up the bank's affairs without further loss to thrifty blacks. His campaign on behalf of federal responsibility for flood control on the Mississippi met with success in 1879. His eloquence in arguing against political disabilities of Confederates won him respect. He was less successful in his pleas to Senators to stop drawing the color line. It was wrong in principle, he said; in addition, it isolated blacks from whites and forced the blacks "against their inclination to act seemingly upon the basis of race prejudice, which they neither respected nor entertained."

One more comment is appropriate. In an era when corruption was rife in the national capital, black Congressmen and Senators adhered to high standards of probity. Former Confederate General Roger A. Pryor reported from Washington that no black Congressman was "in any way implicated in the Credit Mobilier scandal," perhaps the most notorious of the many scandals which beset Congress and the Grant Administration. James G. Blaine, who as a leading Republican politician came to know the Negro Congressional group rather well over a period of years, later wrote, "They were as a rule studious, earnest, ambitious men, whose public conduct . . . would be honorable to any race."

While there may have been no radical changes initiated during Reconstruction, there *were* changes—changes significant enough to appear revolutionary to contemporary Southerners. Change was true of the nation as a whole, of course, but the pace—and therefore the impact—was greater in the South than in the North and West.

In the North and West, rampant economic individualism, industrialization, and urbanization, while taking on new dimensions, were largely continuations of trends that were strong even before the war. People in those sections could cope with the new situation without drastically reorienting traditional habits and attitudes. Further, they had not known military defeat, their lands had been little scarred by war, and their economic strength had grown, not diminished. Emancipation presented few problems to North and West. They continued to segregate blacks, discriminate against them in education, and keep them in the lowest-paid jobs, and, until passage of the Fifteenth Amendment, many states denied black men the right to vote. It is indicative that until the election of Oscar DePriest of Illinois in 1928 to the House of Representatives no Northern community sent a black man to Congress.

In the South, on the other hand, we have seen that Reconstruction meant adjustment to a host of new conditions as a consequence of military defeat. There was still another significant difference between the sections. For at least a generation prior to the war, Northern society had come to accept the principle that individualistic norms must be modified in the interest of social well-being. Gradually, Northerners had come to accept social responsibility in such fields as popular education, mental illness, crime, and care for the poor and infirm. In short, Northern opinion was able to adjust itself to social change with relative slowness.

This was not so true of the South. Native whites, obsessed with the necessity of defending slavery, suppressed criticism of any aspect of the Southern way of life. Such social problems as were admitted to exist were to be met largely through the paternalism of private charity. Some steps were taken in some states to assert social responsibility in education, mental illness, and criminal rehabilitation, but they were feeble and never enjoyed strong public support. Indeed, Southerners generally came to believe with George Fitzhugh that in contrast to the North, with its alleged religious infidelity, social discontent, socialism, and free love, the South was marked by "quiet, contentment, abundance, comfort, conservatism, and religious faith." In such a context, needed social adjustments were bound to be slow. With Reconstruction, social reform, too long delayed, came to the South—in a hurry.

With these specific Southern problems in mind, let us examine the changes ushered in with Reconstruction.

Most obvious was the changed status of the black. No longer property, he was not only a free man but also a free citizen. To an extent undreamed of in the North, black men directly participated in government. At first they were diffident, as when Beverly Nash, a former slave, told the South Carolina constitutional convention: "We are not prepared for this suffrage. But we can learn. Give a man tools and let him commence to use them, and in time he will learn a trade. So it is with voting. We may not understand it at the start, but in time we shall learn to do our duty."

But as black men gained in experience, learned that many white public officials were no better qualified than they, and, in a minor way, shared in the spoils of office, they gained in confidence. This confidence, as well as the political power of the black vote, was reflected in demands for increased black representation in public office. This brought black Republicans into conflict with white office-holders, especially Northerners, for as Reconstruction developed, Southern white and black Republicans, united by a common bond, tended to work against the alien Yankees.

The extent of black participation was impressive. Although blacks were a majority in only one constitutional convention—South Carolina —they helped to write new constitutions in every state of the Confederacy; constitutions under which Southern states continued to function long after Reconstruction was gone, testimony that they were well designed to meet the needs of the section. Negroes sat in every state legislature, although only in the lower house of South Carolina did they command a majority. Elsewhere their proportions in the lower houses (as in 1870–71), ranged from one per cent in North Carolina to nearly 40 per cent in Mississippi. State senates everywhere were predominantly white. Negroes, for the first time in history, also took part in the national legislature. In 1869 three black Congressmen took their seats; their number grew to seven in succeeding Congresses. In the meantime, Mississippi sent two black men to the United States Senate. Countless Negroes were also learning the arts of self-government at the grass roots level, as trial judges, mayors, and sheriffs.

Much has been written in praise of the moderation and conservatism shown by Negroes in public life. It is pointed out that they cooperated with whites in framing the new constitutions. Many opposed disfranchisement of Confederates when numerous whites clamored for it. Blacks did not try to enforce integrated schooling, even when constitutions required it. When corruption became manifest in government they led in the struggle for honesty in office. Many agreed with Beverly

Nash in his avowal that the Southern white man was "the true friend of the black man."

This is all true, but it explains little of black political behavior, apart from the facts that since the outstanding leaders came from the well-to-do and educated elite they tended to be conservative, and that others, feeling their way in a new and strange situation and concerned with keeping white opposition to a minimum, wanted to move slowly.

There was more to it than that.

Black politicians, like their white counterparts, were concerned with power—not power in the abstract, but power to attain certain ends. But whereas white politicians sought ends that were socially acceptable —aid to private enterprise, schools for whites, and the like—black leaders wanted power for ends not yet socially accepted: schools for blacks, civil rights, suppression of racist violence. These men were realists. Despite disclaimers to the contrary, they were rather well prepared to deal with the problems of power. A considerable number of them had received excellent education, either in the North or abroad. Many had been slaves—and who better than a slave knew all the nuances of power? All were the "invisible men" of American society—blacks who, in order to live, had to learn to take advantage of every conscious or unconscious opportunity afforded by white power. In the language of Joel Chandler Harris, they were "Br'er Rabbit" to the white "Br'er Fox."

As realists they realized that they must adapt their means to win their ends in light of the unfavorable circumstances in which they functioned. Except for South Carolina, Mississippi, and Louisiana, blacks were in a minority, and in many places their leadership was undistinguished. In every state, no matter what its black population might be, white power dominated. White racism was rampant, flaring sporadically into violence against outspoken teachers, preachers, and politicians. Northern and Southern Republicans were undependable allies. And until March, 1869, Negroes had to deal with an unfriendly national administration headed by a president who no longer took pains to conceal his aversion to blacks.

As realists they also knew that their counsels of moderation were not universally shared in the black community. Most Negroes were very black and very poor; many of the leaders, especially those most prominent, were light-skinned and wealthy. The distrust that arose from this division reflected itself in suspicion of policies advocated by the elite. There were, however, more immediately cogent reasons for rank-and-file doubt.

The strength of the leadership's appeal lay in their argument that, no matter how much whites might resort to violence against blacks, the hope for Negro progress lay in peaceful political action. But what if peaceful action proved impossible? This theoretical question became practical when an alliance of Conservatives and some Republicans in the Georgia legislature expelled all black members in September, 1868, and followed this up with a resolution declaring black men ineligible for membership. The State Supreme Court declared the action invalid, but there was grave doubt that the legislature would heed the court's decision. Congress then acted, in December, 1869, to compel readmission of the expelled legislators. But the damage had been done. Doubt had been created in the hearts of countless blacks that whites would yield peacefully. The mood was well expressed by Henry M. Turner, a Representative from Bibb County, during the debate on the expulsion resolution. Deriding the conciliatory speeches of other blacks as reminding him "of slaves begging under the lash" he continued:

> The scene presented in this House, today, is one unparalleled in the history of the world. . . . Never [before] . . . has a man been arraigned . . . charged with the offense of being a darker hue than his fellowmen. . . . The Anglo-Saxon race, sir, is a most surprising one. No man has ever been more deceived in that race than I have been. . . . The treachery which has been exhibited . . . by gentlemen belonging to that race has shaken my confidence in it more than anything that has come under my observation from the day of my birth.

Perhaps even more ominous was a growing feeling among militant blacks that protection against white violence lay in resort to arms. In a number of places Negroes had met threatened white force by organizing and arming themselves. In the ensuing confrontations whites had either dispersed or agreed to settle issues by discussion. Negro militants were not slow to draw a lesson.

Black leaders perceived the dangers in such a policy. Large-scale armed confrontation between the races could only endanger the entire black community. To some degree they shared the fear of a Georgia preacher, Charles Ennis, who, in reporting black demands for armed resistance, commented: "I have always told them this would not do; that the whole South would then come against us and kill us off, as the Indians have been killed off." Perhaps more significantly they understood how tenuous was the hold of the black on Northern opinion, and how vulnerable the black would be if native whites could turn that opinion against Southern blacks.

Under all these circumstances, political wisdom called for maneuver, not confrontation. Freedom for maneuver required a policy of moderation: it blunted the edge of native white hostility; it kept Northern opinion favorable; it enabled black men to exploit differences between Northern and Southern Republicans. In short, it provided the means through which black power could be safely asserted.

All this had to be carried through without losing the support of rank-and-file Negroes—or at least, those active in the Negro community. As keenly aware as white politicians of the need for a local power base, black leaders could not afford to alienate black votes. And because they were in a minority position, they sensed, better than many reformers since, that they must not permit the left flank of militants to be detached and destroyed.

Such considerations, together with adherence to principle, explain why moderates, for all their reasonableness, would not give ground on certain issues. Willing to compromise on segregated schools, they won the right for blacks to be educated at public expense. They might make deals on railroad franchises, but they stood firm on civil rights. Even so conservative a man as Francis L. Cardozo took a tough line on civil rights at the South Carolina constitutional convention:

> It is a patent fact that, as colored men, we have been cheated out of our rights for two centuries, and now that we have the opportunity, I want to fix them in the Constitution in such a way that no lawyer, however cunning or astute, can possibly misinterpret the meaning. If we do not do so, we deserve to be, and will be, cheated again. . . .

The demand for protection against white violence was channeled into a successful campaign for state militias, largely manned by Negroes —a development which resulted in great outcries from native whites, as we shall see.

Active black participation in politics helped bring about another major change of Reconstruction—the complete democratization of political life. Reform movements in the pre-war era had brought about increased political participation by whites in many states; in others, especially those on the Atlantic seaboard, oligarchies had managed to keep control of the form as well as the substance of power. The vestiges of aristocratic rule were swept away during Reconstruction. Voting and office-holding were open to all—including Negroes. Some, including educated and well-to-do Negroes, proposed literacy tests for the suffrage—but they were voted down, not only by black but also by poor white votes. State offices were made elective, including some judicial.

Local government was reorganized to make it more responsive to local

needs—and local voters. Juries were open to all; indeed, in South
Carolina it was required that they be constituted racially in proportion
to the number of white and black voters in the county. In the Atlantic
states, where seaboard county oligarchies had long contrived to control
legislatures through an apportionment system which discriminated
against western counties, the new governments provided a more equitable
system of representation.

Accompanying political democratization were beginnings of social
democracy. The pre-war efforts to assert social responsibility in such
fields as education, care for the aged and infirm, relief of poverty, mental
health, and criminal rehabilitation, had been minimal, and what little
success gained had been largely nullified by the war. Thus, in a sense,
Reconstruction meant new beginnings in these significant areas. As we
have seen, the states, backed by enthusiastic black voters, committed
themselves to public education for all—even, in South Carolina and
Mississippi, to providing generous scholarships for needy college students. They also embarked on large-scale programs to provide hospitals
for the mentally ill, special schools for the blind and the deaf, homes
for orphans, and aid to the destitute. To protect the working poor, they
abolished imprisonment for debt, enacted mechanics' lien laws to give
unpaid workmen first claim on a bankrupt employer's assets, and provided exemption for homesteads against seizure by creditors.

The new regimes also took an interest in improving conditions of
other groups suffering from legal and social disabilities. Many states
passed laws extending women's rights in divorce, control of their children, and possession of property. Child welfare laws were enacted to
protect children from brutal parents. The existing legal codes were
modernized and humanized: capital offenses were reduced in number
and barbarous punishments, such as branding with hot irons, outlawed.
Unfortunately, the convict leasing system was left untouched, although
Negro legislators in Georgia made vain attempts to mitigate its abuses.

In these efforts to bring Southern states up to existing Northern
standards, black legislators played a part. In states like South Carolina,
Mississippi, and Louisiana they played leading roles; in others they
helped carry the measures. Samuel J. Lee, Speaker of the South Carolina House of Representatives, modestly summed up their contributions
in 1874: "Every right thinking person must perforce admit that we
have done well. While we are . . . perhaps, very little skilled in the
science of government, many good and laudable enactments have ema-
nated from us."

It is interesting that even hostile white critics paid tribute, if somewhat reluctantly, to black officeholders. James Pike, whose *The Prostrate*

State became a bible for enemies of black power, said of South Carolina legislators: "They have a genuine interest and a genuine earnestness in the business of the assembly which we are bound to . . . respect." Of Mississippi blacks in office, Edward King reported: "There are some who are exceedingly capable, and none of those immediately attached [to the state government] are incapable."

A third major change of Reconstruction due in part to black votes was its setting the stage for the industrialized "New South." No doubt this would have come, sooner or later; the Reconstruction governments hastened its arrival. For industry they offered many advantages, including exemption from taxation for periods ranging up to ten years. For railroads they provided not only franchises but also liberal state aid involving use of state credit, except in Mississippi where the new constitution expressly forbade such action. In the many other ways in which government can influence economic development—licensing, regulation, labor laws, and the like—the Reconstruction governments demonstrated a friendliness to business enterprise which drew no lines between Northerner or Southerner, Conservative or Republican.

Under such benign auspices Southern economic recovery from the war was rapid. As we have seen, production of most agricultural commodities had recovered or had surpassed previous records by 1880. In transportation and industry the record is no less impressive.

During the war the existing rail system of 9,000 miles had taken a beating: maintenance was deferred, rolling stock allowed to wear out, and in many places the roadbed had been destroyed by contending armies. After the war, liberal federal financial aid helped bring about speedy renovation of existing roads, while generous national and state subsidies spurred the building of 7,000 miles of new railroad by 1879.

Industry, benefiting from governmental policies and a public opinion more hospitable than in the pre-war period, surged forward. Between 1860 and 1880 the number of Southern manufacturing establishments rose more than 80 per cent, while the value of their output increased 54 per cent. Cotton mills, owned for the most part by native whites, were particularly profitable. Prior to the collapse of 1873 the industry's average annual dividend was 20 per cent. While Northern mills shut down in the consequent depression, Southern mills continued to operate profitably, providing a return of 8 per cent on invested capital. Tobacco manufacture, another "old" Southern industry, reached a capitalization of $40 million by 1879, thanks in part to promotion of its new product, the cigarette.

New undertakings were initiated in southern Tennessee and northern

Alabama, where the proximity of coal, iron, and limestone made possible the cheap production of steel. Copper mines were opened in Tennessee, while in Lousiana newly discovered sulphur deposits were quickly exploited. By the end of Reconstruction industry was firmly rooted in the old Confederacy.

As industry grew, so did cities. Indeed, the rate of urbanization in the South appears to have exceeded that of the North and West. Richmond, with 38,000 population in 1860 counted 63,000 by 1880; Atlanta grew from 9,500 to 37,400 in the same period; Nashville went from 17,000 to 43,000; and Vicksburg from 4,500 to 11,800. Urbanization meant more active local government, for city dwellers demanded such new services as public sewers and water supply, professional fire departments, and expanded police forces. Local governments were generally responsive, thanks to the democratic reforms carried through by Reconstruction governments.

What did this mean to blacks? To the wealthy elite, it signified opportunities to share, if only in small degree, in the wealth flowing from railroads, mines, and factories. To legislators, it was a chance to partake of the largesse bestowed by promoters on those, be they Republican or Conservative, black or white, who aided their projects. To the black who worked, it meant jobs—jobs which were relatively steady and well paid. Railroad construction, where it was not done by black convicts, called for large numbers of unskilled laborers. In railroad operation many blacks were employed as brakemen and firemen—at wages below those paid whites in similar jobs. The coal and iron mines used blacks, too—unless the work was done by convicts (and they were mostly black). Tobacco shops relied heavily on Negro labor—but there were no jobs for blacks in the cotton mills. From the beginning, the mills had always been lily white.

In housing, black class lines cut deeply. The elite lived in spacious houses in attractive residential areas, displaying, like their white counterparts, all the evidences of conspicuous consumption. Workers were segregated in ghettoes, crowded together in poorly built shanties or tenements, often lacking the public services afforded other areas. The ghettoes, however, did provide opportunities for black merchants and professional people, such as doctors and lawyers. It should be noted that a significant product of Reconstruction was the admission of black men to the bar.

What did Reconstruction mean in terms of improved race relationships? The question is difficult to answer. The direct evidence is scanty, contradictory, and usually so highly subjective as to warrant the utmost skepticism. The indirect evidence is susceptible of contrary interpretations. For example, was the violence employed by whites against blacks a sign of deteriorating relations generally? Or was it an expression of those whites who could not tolerate improving relations between some whites and blacks? It is true that as a result of state civil rights laws and the necessity of whites having to deal with black men in power, people of both races did meet together on an unsegregated basis, and in some places they rode the same street and railroad cars, ate in the same restaurants and stayed in the same hotels—if they had the money. Whether this indicated improved race relationships is another matter.

Nevertheless, there were some signs of change in racial attitudes on the part of some whites. Perhaps the clearest expression of this was an article written in 1870 by Edward A. Pollard, long a spokesman for slavery and the Confederacy. Because of its frank expression of a changing atitude it is worth citing from at length:

> The writer has to confess that he was educated in that common school of opinion in the South that always insisted on regarding the Negro as specifically inferior to the white man—a lower order of human being, who was indebted for what he had of civilization to the tuition of slavery, and who, taken from that tuition, was bound to retrograde and to relapse into barbarism and helplessness. . . .
>
> The South has seen no such thing. . . . [the writer's] former views of the Negro were wrong, . . . this singularly questionable creature has shown a capacity for education that has astonished none more than his former masters; . . . he has given proofs of good citizenship which are constantly increasing; . . . his development since emancipation is a standing surprise to candid observers among the Southern whites themselves; . . . his condition since then has been on the whole that of progress . . . so far from being a stationary barbarian or a hopeless retrograde, the formerly despised black man promises to become a true follower of the highest civilization, a new object of interest to the world, and an exemplary citizen of the South.

The statement is so sweeping as to raise some doubts about Pollard's motives. More significant is the fact that Pollard allowed it to be published. Under Reconstruction fresh winds of change were beginning to blow in the South.

Within the limits set by national Reconstruction policy and the prevalence of *laissez-faire* ideology, Reconstruction in the South seems to have been a qualified success, thanks in considerable degree to active black participation. For the first time in American history black men shared in government as voters, state legislators, Congressmen, administrators, and judges. As such, their record is impressive. They led the campaigns to provide free public education for all children. They helped commit the South to social as well as economic progress. They played a key role in democratizing the political structures of the Southern states, and in providing an almost unparalleled degree of freedom of speech and press.

Despite obstacles, the black masses were slowly acquiring the rudiments of education, and increasing numbers of them were graduating from normal schools, colleges, and universities. Until 1873, jobs were opening up for them in nearly every industry, except cotton textiles. Rural poverty continued to be the rule, but this was only one problem of many which demanded solution. The important element is that during most of the Reconstruction period black men could feel that while problems were by no means solved, the way was open to solve them.

Poor and prosperous whites also shared in the benefits accruing from Reconstruction policies shaped in part by black men. Perhaps in response to this, as well as to civil rights laws and the necessities imposed by having to do business with black men in power, there was a shift in some white attitudes toward blacks, as exemplified in Pollard's essay.

In view of the record, why was this era, so rich in promise in so many fields, brought to an end? Black men had little to do with it. We must, therefore, look to the changing relationships of white Americans, in North and South and West, which had much to do with it. The fate of black Americans was deeply involved, but in the basic decisions made, they held no initiative and had too little voice. Unfortunately for them, black Reconstruction was not that black.

CHAPTER 5

The Withering Away of Reconstruction

Reconstruction formally came to an end on March 4, 1877, with the inauguration of President Rutherford B. Hayes and his immediate withdrawal of remaining federal troops from the South. In fact, Reconstruction had been withering away for years—and two states never experienced it as did others. Tennessee, readmitted before passage of the Reconstruction Acts, passed under Conservative control in October, 1869. When Virginia was restored in 1870 Conservatives were already in power. Georgia presented yet another variation. After the state's readmission in 1868 a combination of maverick Republicans and Conservatives expelled the legislature's black members, as we have seen, and governed until federal intervention. Negroes were not returned to office until January, 1870. Georgia was then readmitted a second time, but within a few months after restoration Conservatives swept into power.

The duration of Reconstruction governments in the remaining states ranged from 34 months (in the case of Texas, the last state to be readmitted) to approximately 8½ years in Florida, South Carolina, and Louisiana. In no case did the Reconstruction governments have sufficient time to establish themselves as viable concerns, particularly in developing among whites new behavior and attitudes toward blacks. In addition to other changes, these governments did suggest new approaches in race relationships, faint though they may have been. That Americans, in all sections, did not follow those suggestions is to be ascribed less to the faults of Reconstruction than to the reluctance of white Americans as a whole to explore the possibilities opened to them. That reluctance helps explain the withering away of Reconstruction.

113

This reluctance stemmed from a number of factors. A basic element was what Thorstein Veblen called "social inertia"—the universal human resistance to change. We Americans pride ourselves on welcoming innovation—and we do, providing it is physical pioneering, as in the West, or technological development, as in the safety razor, the automobile, and television. When changes in social attitudes and behavior are called for, we are much more cautious, as the history of American race relations attests.

There was also present in the post-war generation another element which intensified this resistance to change. During the four years of war the psychological as well as the economic and political capacities of people, both North and South, had been strained to the utmost. With the advent of peace, people yearned for relaxation, for a "return to normalcy," to the familiar way of doing things. That this was impossible, in view of the cultural, economic, and social forces accelerated by or let loose by the war, is beside the point. People *thought* they could return to the familiar past, and passionately desired it. In this, as in so many instances, it was not what the facts were, but what people thought the facts were, that conditioned the course of historical development.

In the North, one expression of this feeling was to write off the black man as a matter of national concern. Many Northerners had never been bothered by the plight of the Negro, but now, even among those who had been disturbed, there were signs of diminished commitment. The mood was well expressed by the veteran abolitionist, Edward L. Pierce, who in 1867 predicted the end of controversy "concerning the African race in this country" because black men were "at last upon their feet, provided with all the weapons of defense which any class or race can have." Earlier, Edward S. Philbrick, the Sea Island plantation superintendent who proved free black labor could be profitable, reported that Bostonians were becoming indifferent to calls for aid to Negro education: "The feeling is somewhat general that the negro must make the most of his chances . . . as he can."

The Northern mood was accentuated by the abolitionists, who now enjoyed a prestige never accorded them before Fort Sumter. In 1870, the American Anti-Slavery Society dissolved itself, proclaiming that adoption of the Fifteenth Amendment completed its mission. Other abolitionist organizations followed suit.

Some Radicals still insisted that the struggle for freedmen's rights was far from over. Thomas Wentworth Higginson, the famed commander of black troops during the war, reiterated his belief that without land the granting of freedom to black men was a "mockery."

Senator Oliver P. Morton of Indiana and Theodore Tilton, editor of the influential weekly, *The Independent*, thought that in its way the Fifteenth Amendment was also a mockery. They argued that it did not guarantee political rights to the black man. Anticipating the later reasoning of the United States Supreme Court in *United States vs. Reese* (1876), they pointed out the amendment merely banned denial of the suffrage on three specific grounds: "race, color, or previous condition of servitude." This, they predicted correctly, would make it possible for Southern states to deny suffrage on grounds other than race. In the words of Senator Morton, "They may perhaps require property or educational tests, and that would cut off the great majority of the colored men from voting in those States and thus this amendment would be practically defeated in all those States where the great body of colored people live."

Morton, Tilton and other Radicals much preferred the original Senate version of the proposed amendment. This was a sweeping affirmation of the American citizen's right to vote by outlawing abrogation of the suffrage because of "race, color, nativity, property, education, or creed."

The ensuing debate brought radical abolitionists into open confrontation with moderates, now joined by the prestigious old-line Radical, Wendell Phillips. The radicals, in the old abolitionist spirit, demanded maximum federal protection for the blacks. The moderates, sensing the temper of the country, were prepared to accept the weaker House of Representatives version as the best they could obtain.

What they could get was limited. Northern states with educational or property voting qualifications would not give them up. Far Western states would accept no amendment enfranchising Chinese. The anti-Negro sentiment which kept voting rights exclusively for whites in many Northern states was very much alive. Such practical considerations doomed the Senate version; the House measure became the Fifteenth Amendment as we know it, in March, 1870.

From the debate and its outcome, Southern Conservatives drew some lessons: the hard-line abolitionists were shrinking in numbers and influence—even the radical Phillips had broken with them; political considerations in North and West compelled even Republicans to follow a moderate line; Conservatives could reasonably expect that in view of such trends they could gain power in the South.

Abandonment of the Negro was the more plausible to many Northern minds because, in their view, there were other and more pressing problems to be met. Immigrants were pouring into the country at an unprecedented rate—nearly 3,240,000 in the ten post-war years. To many Northerners this meant trouble. Political corruption, labor unrest, poverty, crime, slums—all social evils were attributed to the foreigners. In the words of E. L. Godkin, the Irish-born editor of *The Nation*, conservative Northerners believed that if foreigners had been excluded "no changes for the worse, either in government or society, would ever have taken place."

Labor men on the West Coast held much the same view, insofar as it applied to Chinese, of whom 105,000 entered the country in the period, 1866–1875, swelling the number already here. Concentrated in California and the Far West, with their sparse white populations, the very presence of Chinese antagonized whites. The antagonism was intensified by the preference shown by employers, especially railroad contractors, for these industrious and frugal workers who were willing to work for low wages. In 1870 anti-Chinese demonstrations began in California, lynchings followed, and clamor arose for Chinese exclusion, a clamor that became politically potent after the Panic of 1873.

In the nearer West of the Great Plains, the United States had another race problem—the problem that has been with us since early Virginia settlers took over Indian planting grounds. In the Reconstruction era the problem was not with agricultural Indians, but with the nomads of the plains country, whose prime food supply was buffalo. As the transcontinental railroads were built, the buffalo herds were exterminated. The railroads also made it possible for settlers and miners to swarm into lands the Indians thought assured to them by agreements with the United States. Since the United States made little effort to halt the white invasion, and indeed usually furnished military protection when called upon, the Indians fought back. In terms of our day, the Indians believed they were engaged in just wars against aggression waged in violation of solemn pacts and treaties.

Westerners, understandably, did not share this view. The West was theirs, they believed, because their toil and suffering to make it productive gave them moral title, and because God intended the land for those who could make the best use of it—justifications that harked back to the Massachusetts Puritans, who had so sanctified the taking of Indian lands. It was also argued that the Indians were an inferior people, doomed to extinction in competition with whites.

In this light, Indian resistance to white expansion was seen simply as an expression of barbaric savagery, to be put down by any means. Campaigns against Indians frequently became campaigns of extermination, in which women and children as well as warriors were killed.

The justification was succinctly supplied by Colonel John M. Chivington of the Colorado militia: "Nits make lice."

Such actions, when made known back East, caused moral revulsion among people of abolitionist sympathies. Now that the black man had all he could legitimately ask for, in their view, they could turn their energies to helping another oppressed people. Thus the black was supplanted by the red man as an object of Northern white concern. Neither blacks nor whites observed any irony in the fact that so many of the cavalrymen used to extend white power in the West were black.

These developments had a particular bearing on the place of the black man, apart from diverting Northern attention, money, and sympathy from black to red men. Uniting Yankee conservative, West Coast radical, and Great Plains settler, was a common belief in a racial hierarchy. The Yankee believed recent immigrants to be of poorer genetic stock than the Anglo-Saxon. West Coast men, many of them Irish, and thus suspicious of Anglo-Saxondom, held that Chinese were inferior to white men. Great Plains settlers were apt to agree with a major of the Colorado militia who believed "the Indians to be an obstacle to civilization, and should be exterminated." This racism provided a bond of sympathy between many Northerners, Westerners, and Southern Conservatives. When Southerners made their appeals to national opinion they spoke to a public which largely shared their commitment to white supremacy.

There were also more immediate factors which help explain the relegation of the black man to the periphery of white consciousness in the North and West. In the early 70's, Western farmers, squeezed by debt, high interest rates, falling prices, high railroad rates, and the deflationary currency policy followed by the federal government, demanded relief. Through the Grange they organized themselves, entered politics, and became powerful enough in state legislatures to enact the so-called Granger laws in Midwestern states.

Unrest on the prairies was accompanied by dissension in workshops, mines, and factories. Skilled labor organized itself in an effort to halt the inroads of mechanization, which jeopardized both its wage scales and its social status. Thus, the Knights of St. Crispin, made up of shoe craftsmen endangered by the new shoemaking machinery (much of which was due to the inventive genius of the Negro, Jan E. Matzeliger), was organized early in 1867. Already organized groups, such as the Iron Molders, waged strikes, usually without success. Railroad workers, largely unorganized, now formed national unions: in addition to the locomotive engineers, organized in 1863, conductors and firemen founded their own brotherhoods in 1868 and 1873 respectively.

All such efforts met with employer hostility and middle-class suspicion. With the failure of the prolonged molders' strike in 1868, and the demise of the National Labor Union which has previously been discussed, labor made still another attempt to unify its ranks. In 1872 unions banded together in the short-lived Industrial Congress. Earlier, an entirely new union, the Knights of Labor, dedicated to enlisting all labor in its ranks regardless of craft or color, was founded in 1871. Even more disturbing to middle-class opinion were the lurid tales, emanating from the Pennsylvania coal fields, of terror and murder by the alleged "Molly Maguires."

Business, too, had its problems. True, the railroad boom was stimulating the economy, and there were fortunes to be made, as John D. Rockefeller, Jay Gould, Jay Cooke, and innumerable others could testify. But all was not sweetness and light. Bankers wanted hard money and deflation; debtor manufacturers fought for paper money and inflation; iron producers demanded high tariffs on rails; railroad builders preferred cheap imported rails. Woolen cloth manufacturers of New England battled Western wool growers over tariff schedules which limited foreign imports.

Since such struggles involved legislative policy, discussions in Congress came to be dominated by questions of the tariff, public debt, and currency. Increasingly, also, Congress was disturbed by frequent revelations of corruption in its own ranks and in the Federal Administration. The South and the Negro became less and less the object of Congressional attention, although in 1870 and 1871 laws were passed to suppress lawlessness and violence in Southern states. The drift of Congressional sentiment became clear in May, 1872, when a Republican Congress freed all but about 500 Confederates from political restraints previously imposed upon them, while it simultaneously rejected Sumner's attempts to include civil rights amendments to the amnesty.

Symbolic of fading concern for the black man was the fate of the Freedmen's Bureau. Established in March, 1865, as a result of pressure from abolitionists, who perceived the necessity for a period of federal tutelage for the former slaves after emancipation, it represented a compromise between such views and those who held that only an emergency relief operation was necessary.

This reflected a deeper cleavage in outlook. One group, in effect, wanted a social plan, centered on the Negro, involving (for that time) massive federal participation in land reform, education, social welfare, and training for citizenship. The other believed that with freedom the black man should stand on his own feet, just as they believed white men should stand on theirs—a belief expressed by Andrew Johnson in his veto of extension of the bureau in 1866. Congress, he said,

> has never founded schools for any class of our own people, . . . It has never deemed itself authorized to expend the public money for the rent or purchase of homes for . . . the white race who are honestly toiling from day to day for their subsistence. A system for the support of indigent persons in the United States was never contemplated by the authors of the Constitution; nor can any good reason be advanced why, as a permanent establishment, it should be founded for one class or color of our people more than another. . . .

In fact, the abolitionist social planners were too far ahead of their time to win general acceptance either with voters or in Congress. But they were tenacious and they did have sufficient power in Congress to keep the bureau alive and even to extend the scope of services it afforded the Southern black.

They were not strong enough, however, to get adequate finances to enable the bureau to do the job assigned to it. The Congress which set up the bureau appropriated no funds at all for its work, contenting itself with the belief that income from sale or rental of confiscated Confederate public property and of plantations seized by the Union Army would meet the need of caring for millions of destitute whites and blacks. Within six months Andrew Johnson upset this comfortable notion by restoring confiscated lands to pardoned Confederates. In the meantime the Treasury Department had appropriated for its own purposes income from the sale of cotton produced on seized plantations. Later Congresses extended the life of the bureau, and made appropriations which in view of the need and the obligations of the bureau were far from adequate.

One result was that the bureau, set up under the War Department and directed by General Oliver O. Howard, a man of integrity and compassion, was unable to recruit sufficient staff out of its own resources. It then turned to the army to make up the deficiency. Many officers so assigned had to assume the new duties in addition to those for which they were already responsible. Naturally, they were disgruntled—which made for poor morale. In addition, some felt little sympathy for blacks, and some were corrupt, as were some civilians employed as agents. In 1867 the New Orleans *Tribune*, a black newspaper, charged that in the immediate post-war period, "Agents of the Freed-

men's Bureau might have been designated better as planters' agents."
Some military commanders proved uncooperative in executing bureau
decisions. Without such assistance, bureau directives remained dead
letters—which encouraged native white intransigence toward the agency.

Thus, without adequate financing, unable to build a complete civilian
staff of its own, compelled to rely on the cooperation of reluctant military commanders and officers, and subject to the will of Congress, which,
after 1866, seemed unwilling to support it, the bureau staggered along
until 1872, when it was formally ended. In the meantime, many of its
activities had been phased out.

From its beginning the bureau was an object of intense native white
hostility. Its early promise of land for the freedmen not only helped
disrupt the labor supply; it also contributed to the new black sense of
independence, which, to whites accustomed to black submissiveness,
was "insolence." When the hope of land for the landless proved illusory,
the bureau supervised labor contracts between planters and workers.
Although agents were often flagrantly partial to planters, many of the
latter resented even nominal "interference" with their "right" to deal
with labor as they saw fit—a sentiment which would have been shared,
with few exceptions, by every factory owner in the North.

The bureau also set up numerous schools, open to all but attended
mostly by blacks—schools which later became the bases of many public
school systems. To whites, black education they could not control was
dangerous. The courts maintained by the bureau for a time to assure
redress of black grievances—redress impossible in standard white courts
—were seen as penalizing white men in their dealings with blacks.
Then, when Southern Conservatives wooed Northern opinion, bureau
agents disturbed the courtship with reports of outrages against black
and white Republicans. Southern opinion was further aroused because
many bureau agents worked strenuously at building the Republican
party, especially among blacks. This was, of course, anathema! To
whites, this was setting blacks against whites.

In short, the bureau embodied all the hateful features of Yankee
domination; and most hateful of all was its presence as the symbol of
federal protection for black men. It was a measure of growing Southern
Conservative appeal to Northern opinion as well as of declining Northern interest in black men, that the bureau came to an end long before
its mission was accomplished.

In the immediate post-war years, then, Northern support for Southern
blacks declined while sympathy for Southern whites rose. Then came

an event which accelerated both trends—the Panic of 1873 and the ensuing depression, which lasted until 1878. On September 18, 1873, the supposedly thriving banking house of Jay Cooke and Company collapsed. So widespread were Cooke's operations and so unstable the credit structure of the country that in falling he brought the entire economy down with him. Before the depression had run its course— it was the worst in the nation's history to that date—more than 18,000 enterprises failed, including most railroads and more than 420 banks. In 1873 alone the liabilities of failed concerns amounted to $228,000,000. The wholesale commodity price index plummeted from 81 in 1874 to 24.8 three years later—a cold statistical measurement of the distress of farmers and other commodity producers.

They were not alone in their distress. By the winter of 1877–1878 more than three million workers lost their jobs. Congressional pleas for federal aid were rejected as "communistic"; care for the needy was left to private charity at the very time its income was shrinking. Hunger prowled the streets of every American city. As the New York *Tribune* exclaimed early in 1878, "How the unemployed mechanics and laborers have got through this winter, God only knows."

Those fortunate enough to have jobs had to accept lower wages; even so, many jobs were only part-time. Labor, where it was organized, tried to resist. The result was a convulsive wave of strikes in coal mines, textile mills, iron foundries, and elsewhere. The climax came in 1877 with the great railroad strikes, which tied up lines in every part of the country until broken by state or federal intervention. Credulous readers of the press would have believed the country on the brink of revolution. The St. Louis *Republican* averred that these were not strikes at all, but a "labor revolution." The New York *Times* headlined that Chicago was "In Possession of Communists," while its competitor, the *World*, reported Pittsburgh "in the hands of men dominated by the devilish spirit of communism."

Such reporting, a continuation of press treatment of earlier strikes, had its influence in a day when newspapers dominated the communications media: many otherwise sober middle-class citizens genuinely believed they and their country were menaced by red revolution, as James Ford Rhodes, the historian who shared their outlook, documents in his *History of the United States from Hayes to McKinley*.[1] In fact, the unions were so weak and so divided, and their members so poor, that with few exceptions the strikes were unsuccessful and the unions

[1] James Ford Rhodes, *History of the United States from Hayes to McKinley* (New York: The Macmillan Company, 1919), pp. 19–51.

decimated. The number of national unions in existence was reduced from 30 in 1873 to 9 in 1877. Those that survived suffered catastrophic drops in membership.

The strike movement brought into the open once again a source of labor weakness—the exclusion of black men. Although in some places blacks joined with whites in strike action, in many others employers were able to employ hungry blacks as strikebreakers. The short-lived International Labor Union, founded in 1878 by socialists and other radicals, pointed out the vulnerability of labor so long as employers could pit race against race. One of its leaders noted that unless black support was enlisted, "one half of this country must remain adverse or indifferent to our movement." The fledgling Knights of Labor tried to make good its claim to represent all labor: it actively enrolled Negro members. But these were minority movements within a labor minority. Weak as they were, most unionists were not about to give up exclusionist policies. Like Southern Conservatives, Yankee Anglo-Saxons, West Coast Sinophobes, and Great Plains settlers, unionists believed in white supremacy—even when it hurt.

After 1873, then, farmers, workers, and businessmen were all caught up in a literal struggle for survival, a struggle intensified by middle-class fears of impending revolution. Under these circumstances, Northern concern for the black man faded still more, except for a small body of incorrigible abolitionists. Whites desperately trying to save themselves had little patience with those who tried to raise the "nigger question."

There were, however, Northerners to whom the question was a matter of indifference. These were men, who, despite heavy losses, were able to ride out the economic storm; they had sufficient capital, shrewdness, and tenacity to turn disaster into opportunity. With Jay Cooke and many other rivals out of the way, they were able to buy up strategic properties on a falling market. Included among them were August Belmont, financier, American agent of the Rothschild banking house, and active Democrat; Junius S. Morgan, Republican, leading figure in the growing international banking business of the House of Morgan; Anthony Joseph Drexel, the cautious Philadelphia banker whose suspicion of railroad speculation had paid off; Russell Sage, who had helped promote Mount Vernon as a national shrine and later was more profitably engaged in promoting railroads; and his sometime ally, Jay Gould, already notorious as a looter of the Erie Railroad, but who once again demonstrated his ability to land on his feet.

Such men, and others, like Tom Scott, the empire builder of

Pennsylvania Railroad and Collis P. Huntington of the Central Pacific and Southern Pacific, were interested in the South, especially in Southern railroads—and it must be remembered that to the economy of that day railroads were as vital as the automobile industry is to ours. Some, like Belmont and Sage, were already involved and were battling each other for franchises and state aid. Others hoped to profit from difficulties confronting already built Southern lines. Scott and Huntington were preparing for their struggle over control of a projected Southern transcontinental route. To businessmen, political affiliations were unimportant. They would do business with any politician who would do business with them. Their basic requirement was that the politician be in a position to deliver.

After 1873 it was apparent to men of business that the usual policy of working through the Republican party must be modified. Disgruntled voters, blaming the "ins" for their troubles, turned to the "outs." In 1874, for the first time since 1858, Democrats captured control of the House of Representatives—a control they held for six critical years. Two years later, in the famous "disputed election" for the presidency, they outvoted Republicans. To business men interested in the South, the trend was even more clear. In 1873 Texans went Conservative; the next year Alabama and Arkansas joined them; and in 1875 Mississippi followed suit. With four states already in Conservative hands—Georgia, North Carolina, Tennessee, and Virginia—only three remained under Reconstruction governments: Florida, Louisiana, and South Carolina.

Obviously, Northern business men who wanted to operate successfully in the South must deal with Conservatives. Thus, they cultivated—successfully—such Confederate leaders as Jefferson Davis and Alexander H. Stephens, military heroes like Generals Joseph E. Johnston and P. G. T. Beauregard, and Conservative editors, legislators, and other molders of opinion. The Conservatives were better able to deal with the businessmen because the latter came, not as a cooperative and dominating group, but as fiercely competitive rivals, each eager to secure Conservative favors. In such a context the fate of the black man was of little import, except insofar as the Conservatives were committed to white supremacy. This was a minor matter to Northern business men. No more than others less highly placed did leaders of business perceive that the destiny of the nation as a democratic republic was organically linked to that of its black citizens.

If this was not apparent to most whites, it was clear to blacks. As early as 1829 David Walker, the free Negro who made a living as a used clothing dealer in Boston, sounded the warning in his famous *Appeal*:

> . . . Remember, Americans that we must and shall be free and enlightened as you are, . . . Throw away your fears and prejudices then, and enlighten us and treat us like men, and we will like you more than we do now hate you, and tell us now no more about [African] colonization, for America is as much our country, as it is yours.

In the Reconstruction era Isaac Myers reiterated his view that so long as black workers were excluded from the nation's workshops, freedom was meaningless. Frederick Douglass put it in comprehensive social terms in his *Address to the People of the United States* in 1883. Pointing out that blacks were "in every sense Americans," Douglass listed a long series of proscriptions which made blacks a subject people, and concluded:

> We hold it to be self-evident that no class or color should be the exclusive rulers of this country. If there is such a ruling class, there must of course be a subject class, and when this condition is once established, the government of the people, by the people, and for the people, will have perished from the earth.

Doubtless many whites dismissed this in the same spirit as Andrew Johnson had rejected an earlier plea by Douglass: "I do not like to be arraigned by some who can get up handsomely-rounded periods and deal in rhetoric, and talk about abstract ideas of liberty, who never perilled life, liberty, or property." Johnson was both inaccurate and unfair. More to the point is that if Douglass spoke for his people, Johnson spoke for his.

Diminished Northern concern for blacks, rising Northern sympathy for native whites, ambitions of industrial tycoons for Southern expansion, and failure of Northerners to perceive the basic relationship of black and national destinies, do not of themselves explain the success of Southern Conservatives in overthrowing Reconstruction and independent black political power. These were auxiliary forces, contributing to that success, but the basic sources of Conservative strength were in the South; it was there that they fought and won the cold (and sometimes hot) war of Reconstruction. Their rise to power is to be explained largely by factors already discussed—the stresses and strains imposed on a society undergoing rapid transformation after utter defeat in a major war, and Conservative shrewdness in exploiting the possibilities offered by such a situation.

The Conservative drive, rooted in the native white psychology, received unexpected impetus from the Panic of 1873. The benefactions of Jay Cooke and other Northerners to Southern Republicanism dried up, and, as we have seen, Northern survivors of the crash began to court Conservative rather than Republican politicians. Conservatives were also in the advantageous position, in most states, of being "out" when the disaster came, and thus able to intensify their campaign against the "ins"—the Republicans. In states already controlled, they joined their Northern brethren in blaming the policies of the national Republican administration.

The Conservatives were the better able to mount their campaign because distress was as deep and widespread as in the North. The wholesale price of raw cotton, mainstay of the Southern economy as railroad building was that of the North, dropped nearly 50 per cent, from 20.5 cents a pound in 1872 to its low of 10.4 cents in 1879, after a year of national recovery. In the same period sugar prices fell from 12.4 cents to 8.6 cents a pound, and tobacco from 10.7 to 6.1 cents a pound. Turpentine, another Southern staple, went from 61.8 to 31.5 cents a gallon. The general drop in consumer good prices availed little to people overwhelmed by debt contracted at high interest rates. Planters and farmers were dispossessed by the thousands.

Towns and cities were no less affected. As in the North, banks failed, railroads went bankrupt, and although cotton mills continued to prosper other industries felt the chill of economic paralysis. Unemployment was rife, and if hunger was less prominent than in Northern cities, this was largely due to the fact that the mass of Southerners, white and black, lived on the land.

Conservatives could not reasonably blame the Reconstruction governments for what was obviously a national disaster. What they could—and did—argue, was that the Reconstruction governments made a bad situation worse. How? By oppressive taxation, especially on land; taxation which they laid in large measure to governmental corruption. Conservative pledges to reduce taxation by rooting out corruption found eager response, even among some black landowners, who felt the burden perhaps even more keenly than white.

Conservatism, then, attracted followers in all classes of Southern whites and its appeal was strengthened by the Southern plight after 1873. Who were its leaders? What were its aims, apart from overthrow of the Reconstruction governments and restoration of white supremacy?

Perhaps the most striking feature of the men who evoked the symbols of the traditionalist South is that few were traditionalists. For the most part they were identified with the "new men" of the South, eager to shift from a purely agrarian to a diversified economy, dominated by business—railroading, manufacturing, mining, banking. In that sense they were willing to remake the South in the Yankee image, and indeed they cooperated with Northern capitalists engaged in extending their economic domain through the South. But economic development must be in Southern hands, insofar as that was possible, given the shortage of Southern capital; native whites must have representation in Northern enterprises; and to assure that (as well as for other reasons) native white political control must be restored.

In this way, it was argued, industrialization of the South would benefit both those directly engaged in promoting it and the people of the South as a whole. In pursuing these ends Conservatives were willing to overlook past political heresy. Thus, the native white Republican Chief Justice of the Georgia Supreme Court, Joseph E. Brown, was welcomed to the councils of the faithful, and became a pillar of Conservative strength in post-Reconstruction Georgia.

A brief review will indicate how much Conservative leaders were committed to the new order:

John C. Brown, first Conservative governor of Tennessee, was an ally of Tom Scott in his railroad empire building, became a vice-president of Scott's company, the Texas and Pacific, and later was president of the powerful Tennessee Coal, Iron and Railroad Company, a major beneficiary of the convict leasing system.

John B. Gordon, hero of Lee's last campaign, later Governor of, and United States Senator from, Georgia, was actively involved in coal mining enterprises even before the war. He was an ally of Collis P. Huntington of the Central and Southern Pacific Railroads, in the westerner's battles with Scott for control of a southern route to the west coast. Later he was identified with the Louisville and Nashville Railroad and was active in various insurance, manufacturing, and real estate companies.

Lucius Q. C. Lamar of Mississippi collaborated with Gordon in some of his business ventures and accumulated wealth as a corporation lawyer. A Congressman during the Reconstruction era, he became chairman of the Pacific Railway Committee and fought to get federal subsidies for the Northern Pacific and the Texas and Pacific projects. In the post-Reconstruction era his stand for the hard-money policy favored by banking interests earned him the distrust of Mississippi farmers.

Wade Hampton of South Carolina, owning extensive plantations in his native state and in Mississippi, was the embodiment of the patrician tradition. He was also a glamorous hero of the Lost Cause: in addition to dramatic military exploits, he had rejected Southern surrender, proposed continued resistance from Texas, and tried to join the fleeing Jefferson Davis. Even he was attuned to the new order. As governor in the post-Reconstruction era he sided with bankers over attempts to control lending rates, with bondholders in quarrels over the state debt, and with railroads in their fight against regulation.

As noted earlier, some Conservative leaders had been former Whigs and other Democrats. They were bound together now not only by their belief in white supremacy but also by a social and political philosophy which, while it served their ends, also promoted the interests of section and nation—or so they professed. This was an updated Whiggism, still concerned with protecting property rights and recognizing class distinctions in society, but now buttressed with the teachings of Herbert Spencer. These held that social progress was the outcome of an inevitable individualistic "struggle for existence," out of which came the "survival of the fittest." Such a philosophy, decked out with the trimmings of nineteenth century science, had obvious appeal to successful men of the "robber baron" era.

It had another appeal to Southern Conservatives. Just as there was competition between individuals, so there was competition between races. Since black men were by nature inferior, they were incapable of meeting the demands of a competitive society. If the black man were to survive at all, he must be confined to the menial tasks for which nature destined him. For his own well-being he must be relegated to subordinate status, in which white society would protect him from the harsh realities of the struggle for existence. Black men might not believe him, but the Conservative was persuaded, as one leader put it, that white supremacy would secure "the welfare and happiness of the African."

It should be noted that while Conservatives denounced federal action on behalf of black men on the ground that it interfered with the "natural" relation of the races, they welcomed governmental intervention in the "struggle for existence" when it came in the form of railroad subsidies or other aids to business. This provided a common meeting ground for Southern Conservatives and Northern businessmen, such as August Belmont of the Louisville and Nashville railroad and those competitors for Southern favor, Tom Scott and Collis P. Huntington. It was to prove of great moment in bringing black political power to an end.

In their campign to overthrow Reconstruction governments Conservatives enjoyed certain basic advantages.

Collaboration with Northern business interests was profitable in political as well as in economic terms. Such Yankees had close working relations with leading politicians of both parties. They also either owned newspapers or were on familiar terms with such powerful independent editors of the day as Joseph Medill of the Chicago *Tribune,* James Gordon Bennett of the New York *Herald,* and Charles A. Dana of the New York *Sun.* Through the Yankees Southern Conservatives gained access to Northern opinion and to the councils of the major parties—although in the case of the Democrats it was extension of existing Southern influence rather than a new departure. In any case, the Yankee connection gave Conservatives more political leverage at the national level.

While Conservatives gained an opening to Northern opinion, their appeal to native white opinion was growing, not only because of their message but also because of who they were—white Southerners, born and bred in the Southern white tradition, speaking the Southern tongue and voicing in familiar terms Southern conscious aspirations and unconscious drives.

Overshadowing all was the mighty moral authority of Lee. Although he refrained from politics, it became known that the great hero of the Confederacy thought Republican Reconstruction policy not "the one best for the interests of the country." In counselling active political participation to his fellow Virginians he sounded the essential Conservative note of white unity to rid themselves of Republican governments: "I am confident that, if we all unite in doing our duty, and earnestly work to extract what good we can out of the evil that now hangs over our dear land, the time is not distant when the angry cloud will be lifted from our horizon. . . ." Unfortunately for Southern Republicans, there was only one Lee—and the Conservatives had him.

Other Conservative advantages flowed from the national Reconstruction policy. Failure to provide land for the freedmen made blacks vulnerable at the point of most effective pressure: their ability to make a living. As blacks had long insisted, their lack of land made them subject to those who had it—a fact equally well appreciated by native whites. Further, the decision to reconstruct the Union on the basis of the old state structure provided means whereby Conservatives could capture control state by state with little fear of federal intervention. Finally, the practice of national and state governments in permitting free expression of opinion and freedom of political organization— presumed American rights long suppressed in the pre-war South— facilitated the work of Conservatives, although, as we shall see, their efforts were not confined to legal means.

Despite these advantages, the Conservative road to power was far from clear.

There was the tricky problem of winning over the mass of poorer whites. They were numerous, and thanks to Reconstruction constitutions, exercised an unprecedented amount of political power. Farmers and mechanics had long distrusted Southern Whiggery; they were little less suspicious of the new breed of Southern business men who consorted with Yankee millionaires and sometimes spoke of Negro "rights." They might respect a Lee; they also knew how honest men could be misused by shrewd rogues. And no small number of them had opposed the war, especially in the mountain areas, not because they liked the black man but because they hated the plantation system.

To be successful, Conservatives had to bridge this class division, and bridge it in such a way that they could take power while denying it to the white poor. Their response to the problem took several forms. Friendship with Yankee tycoons was explained away with assurances that it would bring industry and prosperity to the South. Such economic growth would benefit all Southerners, particularly since Southern men would have a significant voice in how Northern capital functioned in the South. Promotion of the cult of the Lost Cause helped unite whites, regardless of class, in a transcendent sectional patriotism.

Most potent in the Conservative appeal, of course, was invocation of the cause not yet lost—white supremacy. For tactical reasons some major Conservative leaders, such as Wade Hampton in South Carolina and John McEnery in Louisiana, made overtures to Negroes and pledged respect for black rights. Grass-roots leaders assured their followers not to take this too seriously. In the words of one such leader, real Conservative policy was to treat blacks so as to impress them "that their natural position is that of subordination to the white man."

But the white supremacy issue could not be pushed too far, lest it permanently alienate the black vote, for some political strategists perceived that in the event of Conservative victory a properly controlled black vote would be useful in counteracting poor-white votes. Thus, Conservatives strove to unite native whites behind the program of

white supremacy while they also tried to provide sufficient evidence
of friendship to black men so as to divide and disarm them in the
immediate political situation.

There were other hazards in the white supremacy campaign. Northern
interest in the Negro had diminished, but it had not disappeared—
any flagrant assault on Negro rights brought outcries for federal intervention. In addition, black men's rights still provided useful campaign
ammunition for Northern Republicans, tied in with "bloody shirt"
appeals to memories of the war, as useful in their way as invocations
of the Lost Cause were in the South. So, Conservatives must avoid
an outright attack on black men's rights; at the same time, they must
not appear so friendly to black men as to lose poor white men's votes.

Besides, the South needed and needed badly, federal aid for public
works projects ranging from flood control on the Mississippi to making
war-damaged harbors and rivers once more navigable. Unfortunately
for the South, innumerable communities in North and West thought
themselves in equally bad plight. In the ensuing competition for
limited federal funds Northern Democrats were as zealous as Republicans in promoting the interests of their own constituencies. The
resulting neglect of Southern needs provided good campaign fodder for
Conservatives, but the communities involved were less interested in
campaign slogans than in increased federal aid. And this aid would
not be forthcoming were Northerners to be furnished a Southern race
issue.

Southerners also were deeply concerned about getting a transcontinental railroad route linking their cities with the Pacific. This meant
obtaining federal charters and federal subsidies. On this issue there
was not only sectional competition but other vexing complications.
After the exposure of the Credit Mobilier scandal in 1872 Northern
Democrats, finding railroad subsidy corruption a mighty club with
which to beat Republicans, were hostile to further subsidies—even those
which benefited their Southern associates. Their attitude seemed to
block Southern hopes—but there were two men who were sure the
road would be built and each of whom was determined that the road
was going to be his: Tom Scott and Collis P. Huntington. This put
Conservatives in an advantageous position for bargaining, but it also
placed them in the center of a titanic battle for power—and Conservatives could afford to alienate neither titan.

Under all these circumstances—the distrust of the poorer whites, the
political power of the blacks, the value of Southern race issues to
Northern Republicans, the need for federal aid for Southern public
works and railroads—it behooved Conservative leaders to tread warily.

Equally, they had to exploit any opening in the opposition, take advantage of every opportunity offered, to carry out their strategy of white supremacy, with some whites more supreme than most. This involved neutralizing, undermining, and eventually destroying, black political power, except under those conditions where it could be manipulated in the Conservative interest.

If the black man has appeared only peripherally in this discussion, it is not because he was passive—for he was not—but because he had little voice in making the basic decisions which were to shape his future. Those decisions were made for him by white men—abolitionists, Western farmers, labor union members, Northern bankers and industrialists. Most of them believed in white supremacy. In granting formal civil and political equality to the black man, they felt they had done all that could be reasonably expected of them. More, such equality, by providing conditions for equality of opportunity, made it possible for Negroes to prove themselves as individuals and as a race.

This, of course, was an abstraction. It ignored the context in which the black man functioned: overwhelming poverty and illiteracy, the still festering psychological wounds of slavery, and the hostility of Southern white society to the very notion of Negro equality. Ignoring the context meant that in practice the abstraction became a means through which the fate of the Southern black was determined by Southern Conservatives, who had long since decided that the proper status for black men was that of subordination.

CHAPTER 6

Uprooting Black Power

The Conservative campaign to uproot black power employed both legal and illegal means. The former comprised propaganda appeals directed at Northern opinion combined with wooing of Northern business interests, rallying Southern white opinion under the banner of white supremacy, and organization of political opposition to the Reconstruction governments. The latter embraced varied forms of terrorism directed against black and white Republicans. Since the terrorism had the tacit—and sometimes open—support of most native whites, it was widespread, except in those periods when federal power was invoked to suppress it.

The appeal to Northern opinion centered on racism and corruption. The basis of Northern racism we have already discussed; its strength was attested to by Republican strategy in the presidential election of 1868. Although their candidate was the "savior of the Union," U. S. Grant, Republicans ran scared. Negro suffrage, imposed on the South, had been recently rejected by white voters in several Northern states, and Democrats had made sensational gains in the 1867 state elections. Republican failure to oust Andrew Johnson through impeachment in May, 1868, had heartened Democrats in both North and South. During the campaign the Democratic nominees, former governor Horatio Seymour of New York and former Republican Congressman Francis P. Blair of Missouri, bid for white support by picturing the dangers of alleged black domination under Reconstruction and calling for "restoration" of white rule in the South.

Northern Republicans responded with their own brand of racist appeal. They assured Northerners that black voting as a matter of national policy was limited to the South; in the North, voters were free to accept or reject it. Besides, they pointed out, Republicans in Congress had rejected proposals that Southern states be required to guarantee the civil rights of black men before admission to the Union. Republicans also exploited Northern white fears by emphasizing that continued white terrorism in the South, which Northern newspapers reported in detail, could lead to an exodus of blacks to the North. If white men wanted to avoid this, they should support the Republicans and their Reconstruction policy—which would keep black men in the South.

Democrats lost the election, but Southern Conservatives noted that both parties had found it expedient to cater to white feeling about blacks.

Conservatives set out to cultivate that white sentiment. They made good use of Congressional hearings on Southern violence, projecting, through witnesses, the image of a sorely tried people, beset by unscrupulous Northern adventurers, threatened with black violence, the women prey to black rapists. Through the minority reports of Northern Democrats on such committees they obtained what advertising men today would call favorable national exposure of their political wares.

Perhaps the best example of the use of this technique was that of John B. Gordon of Georgia, Klan leader, "new man" of Reconstruction, and later political boss of his state for a generation. In testimony before a Congressional committee in 1871 he disclaimed all knowledge of the Klan except for what he read in the newspapers, but conceded that in 1868 he had joined a secret society of "the property-holders, the peaceable, law-abiding citizens of the state, for self-protection." It was nonpolitical and non-violent, he asserted.

Why was it organized? Because carpetbaggers, operating through the Union Leagues

> were organizing the colored people. . . . We knew of certain instances where great crime had been committed; where overseers had been driven from plantations, and negroes had asserted their right to hold the property for their own benefit. . . . Men were in many instances afraid to go away from their homes and leave their wives and children, for fear of outrage. Rapes were already being committed in the country. There was this general organization of the black race on the one hand, and an entire disorganization of the white race on the other hand. . . .

Northern Democrats took up the Conservative cry. They echoed Southern charges against the Freedmen's Bureau, especially that it had misled and corrupted "ignorant" blacks. Democrats on the joint committee investigating Southern outrages in 1871 condemned the crimes of the secret societies, but denied that these had "any general organization, or any political significance, or that their conduct is endorsed by any respectable member of the white people in any State." However, they continued, it should be remembered

> that no people had ever been so mercilessly robbed and plundered, so wantonly and causelessly humiliated and degraded, so recklessly exposed to the rapacity and lust of the ignorant and vicious portion of their own community and of the other States, as the people of the South have been. . . . History, till now, gives no account of a conqueror so cruel as to place his vanquished foes under the dominion of their former slaves. . . .

A major value of such reports lay in their being reported throughout the nation, and thus helping create a favorable climate of opinion for the Conservative viewpoint.

This was clear in 1876 in the Democratic minority report on the Senate investigation into the Mississippi state election of 1875. After repeating allegations about "property and intelligence" being ground under the heel of the "most ignorant and sometimes vicious members of the community," the Democrats, with an eye to Western sentiment, made a frankly racist appeal:

> the relations of the African to the white race in the United States do not stand alone for consideration; . . . on our Pacific coast the dark shadow of an Asiatic horde hangs lowering over the white population, and has aroused their gravest apprehensions.

The Fifteenth Amendment, said the Democrats, by barring race as a qualification for suffrage, opened "to the teeming oriental populations unobstructed opportunity, by their mere number, to control our elections, and our Governments, State and Federal."

In such manner Southern Conservatives and Northern Democrats sought to fuse racist feelings throughout the nation into a common body of sentiment which would hasten the end of black power.

In addition to racism, Conservatives had another string to their bow in reaching national opinion—the issue of corruption. Corruption, it must be understood, was nothing new in national life. As early as 1787 the Rev. Manasseh Cutler, little in the odor of sanctity, had maneuvered through Congress a measure for the Ohio Company providing 1,500,000 acres of choice public lands for the company at eight cents an acre. Other scandals had occurred intermittently, as during the passage of Alexander Hamilton's funding measures and in the corruption associated with the Bank of the United States in the 1830's. During the Civil War Washington was infested with "influence peddlers" who labored with politicians and administrators on behalf of their contractor clients.

Nor was corruption unknown in Southern politics. In 1795, the Georgia legislature, suitably bribed, had sold for a cent an acre most of the state's western public lands, embracing most of what are now the states of Alabama and Mississippi. The state of Mississippi repudiated its own bonds following the Panic of 1837: a basic reason was the nation-wide economic collapse, but an immediate factor was that many tax collectors pocketed much of their collections. During the war "influence peddlers" and speculators were no less active in Richmond than in Washington.

Corruption was not new—what was new was the growth of a formidable body of opinion in the North which found it intolerable, and the Southern Conservative perceived that here was a means of enlisting support from men who might be immune to the cruder sort of racist appeal. The Northern men, who believed that "public office is a public trust," had unimpeachable credentials as men of personal integrity, staunch Unionists, and "friends" of the black man.

They included Charles Francis Adams, Jr., scion of the Adams dynasty that reached back to John Adams, second President of the United States; Carl Schurz, the German immigrant who had made himself a power in Republican politics while building a reputation for rectitude; Horace Greeley, abolitionist editor of the New York *Tribune*; Charles W. Eliot, the young president of Harvard; and E. L. Godkin, editor of *The Nation*, which to numerous middle-class Americans as well as to historian James Ford Rhodes, its devoted reader, was the expression of "civilization and good political morals."

Such men felt the nation endangered by the flouting of morality in the unscrupulous rush for wealth in the post-war era. There was not only a collapse of private morality, shown by the Erie and Union Pacific railroad scandals. There was also a decline in civic morality. Boss Tweed, with seeming immunity, was looting New York—his total take of more than $100 million is estimated to have exceeded the corruption in all the Southern states together. His was only one of many "rings" operating in Northern and Western states and cities. Rumors of corruption touched even the White House!

To this sentiment, Conservatism made its appeal. Southerners, too, were protesting against unconscionable corruption. They presented evidence of mounting state debt and rising taxes, which, they asserted, were grinding decent white people into poverty and despair. Where was the money going? Into the pockets of crooked Republican politicians, white and black, but especially carpetbaggers, Northern men of low antecedents who had no interest in the South save to loot it before retiring in affluence to the North. Also of importance in the Conservative argument was the charge that the legislatures were made up largely of poor men, white and black, who paid little or no taxes and thus felt no pain in levying taxes on property owners. This made manifest appeal to Northern middle-class voters.

The Conservative case was selective, of course. The debt figures were highly inflated, including not only actual but also contingent state indebtedness. The latter arose out of state aid given railroad promotions in the form of bonds secured by liens against the properties involved. These would become claims against the state only when and if the state took over the railroad to which aid had been given. Also, much of the actual debt—and taxes—arose from the need of Southern states to rebuild plant and equipment destroyed by the war and from their expansion into new areas of public responsibility, such as popular education. These factors were rarely mentioned in Conservative testimony.

Nor did Conservatives tell the whole story of Southern corruption. They said little of the Conservative public officials, who, during the Johnson government era, filched public funds in Mississippi and Alabama. They were reticent about the notorious Louisiana Lottery. The lottery, chartered by a Republican legislature, was a native white enterprise, and numbered among its beneficiaries many Conservatives.

Under Reconstruction, Conservatives were out of power, and thus could share little in the mulcting of public treasuries, but as seekers of legislative and gubernatorial favors they were no more backward than Yankees in using the persuasion of the greenback. For example, some South Carolina businessmen, conservative in politics, spent $40,000 in obtaining from the legislature a profitable monopoly in mining phosphate, used in the production of fertilizer. In Georgia, Conservative leaders worked with Hannibal I. Kimball, Yankee railroad promoter, in a corrupt scheme through which they obtained a highly favorable lease of a state-owned railroad. In Alabama, the struggle between rival groups of railroad promoters involved Conservative as well as Yankee bribery of legislators.

Immersed as they were in corruption, Conservatives dared not push the issue too hard; as an Alabama Conservative wrote later, they must be careful lest they be confronted with "embarrassments of no ordinary magnitude." Such considerations may explain, in part at least, the reluctance of Conservatives, once in power, to bring accused men to trial, and the acquittal of many who were brought into court.

The basic political motivation of the corruption issue was indicated by the fact that honest Republican administrations were not immune to Conservative subversion. The administration of Adelbert Ames, remarkable in Mississippi politics for its financial integrity, was toppled in a violent Conservative campaign, as was that of Daniel H. Chamberlain in South Carolina. Chamberlain had so cleaned up corruption and inefficiency in state government that a minority of Conservatives wanted to support him in 1876!

At the time, however, Conservative arguments made headway. Northern newspapers gave space to Conservative claims. Some, like the New York *Tribune*, which had been sympathetic to Reconstruction, became increasingly hostile. This was true also of such influential journals as *The Nation* and *Harper's Weekly*. Northern opinion was also influenced by the reports of leading newspapermen, like James S. Pike and Charles Nordhoff. Nordhoff's reports were more restrained than the sensational accounts of Pike, but both gave aid and comfort to the Conservative cause.

The major breakthrough in the Conservative effort to woo Northern sentiment came in 1872. In that year reform elements in the Republican party set up their own Liberal Republican organization, chose Horace Greeley as their candidate, and adopted a platform consistent with the Conservative program for the South.

It called for "universal amnesty" for Confederates. Local government was held to be a better safeguard of individual rights than "any centralized power." Restoration of "state self-government" was demanded. Federal laws against Southern violence were obliquely attacked by challenging the use of military power and suspension of the writ of *habeas corpus*—both authorized under the Ku Klux Klan law of 1871.

If there was doubt in some minds as to the meaning of some of the platform's generalities, Greeley's New York *Tribune* dispelled it. Greeley's election, it said, would mean "reconciliation with the South, an end of the war, a revival of Southern industry, increased markets for Northern products, a homogeneous country, with consequent safety and prosperity." It would also signify, said the *Tribune*, "an end of carpetbag governments at the South, propped up by Washington interference for yet longer robbery of already bankrupt communities."

The Liberal Republican bid for power failed. Even so, Southern Conservatives could count substantial successes. For the first time their cause had been taken up by a Northern party to which no taint of "rebellion" attached, and while the effect of this had been somewhat diminished by the Democratic endorsement of Greeley, it remained true that Southern Conservatism had attained a new level of respectability in the North.

Also, the Conservative version of Southern corruption and oppression under "Negro-carpetbag" rule, together with endorsement of the Conservative demand for "restoration of home rule," were expounded in countless towns and villages by Northern men, such as Greeley and Schurz, whose patriotic credentials were beyond question. And numerous editors, sympathetic with Liberal Republicanism, hammered at Reconstruction policies almost as much as they attacked "Grantism." In short, the beachhead established by Conservatism in Northern opinion was rapidly expanded by reputable Northern men—a process continued with the work of Pike and Nordhoff.

Beyond that, the 1872 campaign represented the opening of large-scale dialogue between "intelligence and property" of the North and their Southern counterparts, a dialogue which would take on new dimensions after the Panic of 1873. Obviously, it was a dialogue from which black men were excluded.

The rapprochement between white North and white South portended in the long run the end of Reconstruction; in the short run it inhibited federal action on behalf of black men. This became apparent in 1872, when a combination of Democrats and Liberal Republicans blocked in the House of Representatives a Senate proposal to extend a key section of the law of 1871 directed against Southern terrorism— a section that was about to expire. The Democratic triumph in the 1874 elections hastened the process, as was evident in the Grant Administration's response to the critical situation which developed in Mississippi during the state elections of 1875.

Heartened by the Democratic national victories, white Mississippians decided on drastic action to carry their state for Conservatism, under the slogan, "Carry the election peaceably if we can, forcibly if we must." Peaceful measures were by no means ignored, but the emphasis was on force. Scores of blacks were killed, Negro office-holders were compelled to flee, and voters were so frightened they dared not meet. Black appeals for aid flowed into Governor Ames' office, summed up in one such: "our lives are not safe, . . . and therefore we deem it unwise to make a target . . . to be shot down like dogs and have no protection." Ames strove to restore order, but the whites were openly defiant. In desperation, Ames called on Washington for aid. Here surely was a situation much worse than that of South Carolina in 1871 when Grant had dispatched troops and suspended the writ of *habeas corpus.*

But times had changed. Businessmen high in the councils of the Republican party, such as Tom Scott and Grenville Dodge, were working together with Southern Conservatives to bring off their railroad schemes. Northern voters had shown their disenchantment with the Republicans by their votes in 1874. Businessmen and practical politicos were both arguing that Republican identification with Negro rights was hurting the party in the North. Indeed, at the moment Ames' appeal reached Washington, Ohio Republicans were warning Grant that sending troops to Mississippi would cost the party that key Northern state in the upcoming state elections.

Besides—and this is symbolic in itself—Grant had a new attorney general, Edwards Pierrepont of New York, an avowed foe of Reconstruction who had been a Democrat until he joined the Republicans in 1868. Exclaiming that "The whole public are tired of these annual autumnal outbreaks in the South," Pierrepont persuaded Grant against intervention. As Ames observed later, Grant's failure to move revealed that the executive branch had written off Reconstruction as a "failure." That political fact of life was also apparent to Southern Conservatives.

What was true of the executive was little less true of the judicial branch. While it circumspectly avoided outright challenge to Reconstruction, the Supreme Court's attitudes reflected little concern for black men's rights. As noted earlier, its decision in *ex parte Milligan* (1866) aroused indignation among Radicals and abolitionists because it called into question much of the legal basis of federal protection for freedmen. With the passage of the Reconstruction amendments, such friends of the black man were confident they had put his welfare beyond the reach of hostile courts and legislatures.

But constitutional amendments are not self-enforcing. They require enabling legislation, and this Congress provided in a body of law designed to make the amendments effective. Such legislation, however, is subject to judicial scrutiny—and thus the Supreme Court was afforded an opportunity not only to review the laws but also to interpret the amendments from which the laws drew their authority.

Through this process the Court, during the 1870's, annulled those parts of the laws most effective in protecting black rights, and so limited by interpretation the Fourteenth and Fifteenth Amendments as to render them, for a long time, irrelevant to the welfare of black Americans.

During those years, the Court, no less than other institutions, was adapting to changing circumstances—symbolized in its changed personnel. Chief Justice Salmon P. Chase, that erratic friend of the black man, died in 1873. His place was taken by Morrison R. Waite, an Ohio Republican who soon showed he shared little of Chase's views. Earlier—in 1870—Grant had appointed to the Court Joseph P. Bradley, New Jersey corporation lawyer, whose dubious behavior as circuit judge made it possible for Tom Scott to acquire at little cost the valuable properties and land grants of a defunct Southern railroad and later led to the accusation that he was "Tom Scott's man." Grant's two other appointees, William Strong of Pennsylvania and Ward Hunt of New York were lawyers typical of the "new" Republicanism, dedicated to the interests of business and little concerned with the problems of the poor, white or black.

Like the old, the "new" Court did not challenge outright the Reconstruction legislation. What it did was to erode, not simply the legislation, but the very premises on which the Fourteenth and Fifteenth Amendments were based. In 1873, the Court passed on a Louisiana statute granting a monopoly to a slaughterhouse company in New Orleans on grounds of public health. Competitors challenged this, claiming their rights had been abridged under the Fourteenth Amendment.

The Court, over which Chase still presided, held that the amendment was meant to apply to problems of black citizens, but it also set forth the rule that there was a distinction between national and state citizenship and held that certain basic rights "belong to citizens of the states as such, . . . they are left to the state governments for security and protection, and not [by the Fourteenth Amendment] placed under the special care of the federal government." A little more judicial interpretation on this line and the protection of black rights would be left to the states, as soon appeared.

Such a step was taken in 1875 in the case of a Missouri woman who claimed her rights under the Fourteenth Amendment were violated under state law restricting suffrage to men. The Court disagreed. Holding that "The United States has no voters in the States of its own creation," the justices declared the right to vote derived from state, not national citizenship, and was properly subject to state regulation. The unanimous decision underscored this by asserting that "the Constitution of the United States does not confer the right of suffrage upon any one."

The following year the Court stripped the Reconstruction amendments of much of their significance to black men. In *United States vs. Reese* it knocked out key provisions of federal legislation designed to protect Negro suffrage and went on to interpret the Fifteenth Amendment in a purely negative fashion. The amendment, said the Court, did not guarantee the citizen's right to vote; it simply prohibited denial of that right on specific grounds of race, color, or previous condition of servitude. Otherwise, qualifications for voting rested with the states. Thus the way was left open for Southern states later to legally disfranchise blacks on grounds ostensibly other than race.

In *United States vs. Cruikshank* the Court was presented squarely with the problem of Southern white violence against Negroes. It was asked to pass on indictments against Louisiana whites accused of attacking a Negro meeting and conspiring to deprive blacks of their political rights—both federal offenses under existing legislation. The Court threw out the indictments on the ground that the legislation was not authorized under the Fourteenth Amendment. The amendment, said the court, did not take from the states their responsibility to protect the basic rights of their citizens: "That duty was originally assumed by the state; and it still remains there." With this magnificent abstraction the Court turned over to native whites the protection of black rights.

Thus, by 1876 the Supreme Court had effectively destroyed the structures through which abolitionists had fondly hoped to help the black man find meaning in freedom. In this the Court reflected the trend of opinion and events. Northern opinion, the Congress, and the Executive had written off the black man as a major national concern. It remains to explain how Conservatives destroyed black power where it had indigenous strength—in the South.

The fundamental appeal to Southerners was white supremacy. In addition, Conservatives raised the intertwined issues of corruption and high taxation, which they astutely ascribed to the corruption of the Republican regimes while they equally astutely obscured their own role. Besides, they alleged, the taxes were voted by legislators who owned little or no property; that is, the have-nots were disposing of the property of the haves. This was not accidental, they pointed out. Some outspoken lawmakers, including blacks, advocated high taxation not simply on fiscal grounds but also on grounds of social policy. They hoped that such taxation would result in the break-up of large estates and encourage more widespread ownership of land—an end which Thomas Jefferson would have found eminently in keeping with his ideal of a land of small independent farmers. Unfortunately, few black men had the cash or credit to take advantage of such a policy.

The Conservative argument had strong appeal to men whose estates were threatened, and their number was not small, although they might not be the men who owned the estates in 1865. Since that time Yankees and Southern "new men" had acquired many plantations from impoverished planter aristocrats. To smaller landowners the argument also appealed, for they operated on a much smaller margin than the wealthy planters. Sharp rises in taxation—given the decline in Southern commodity prices—meant to them not simply a shrinking of capital, as in the case of the wealthy, but threats to their very existence as independent proprietors. Even to tenants there was point to the case, for landlords tried to pass along higher taxes in the form of higher rents or other charges. Since so much of Southern society was agrarian, the linked issues of corruption and taxation were a major influence.

Conservative charges emphasized black responsibility for corruption. Black votes were sold, of course—but so were white, and the white price was higher. In Florida, for example, white legislators commanded from $2,000 to $6,000 for their votes, while blacks had to be content with $500 or less. Similar situations existed in other states—in corruption as in everything else, a color line was drawn. Little was said about black incorruptibles such as Francis L. Cardozo of South Carolina and Oscar J. Dunn of Louisiana. Indeed, it was said of the latter that a reason why he was held in such distaste by native whites was because he could not be bribed!

Reasons for black corruption are not far to seek. Many black officials were very poor indeed—the addition of a few hundred dollars a year to their income meant the difference between penury and comfort. Besides, corruption was so rife as to be almost typical—and it was engaged in by some of the best men of white society as well as some of the worst. Whites provided few models of probity in public affairs. In addition, corruption was often involved in matters in which the average black official had little concern—granting of franchises and other favors to businessmen. If white men wanted to pay the black man for his vote in such affairs, why shouldn't the black man accept? There was also, perhaps, another element involved in black psychology, revealed in an explanation allegedly given by a bribed Negro legislator: "I've been sold in my life eleven times . . . and this is the first time I ever got the money."

On another front, Conservatives identified themselves with the cause of economic progress—a cause no less sacrosanct in the South than in the North and West. In collaboration with Northerners they were to the fore in developing coal and iron mines, in the process opening profitable careers for professional men, merchants, and real estate speculators. Even more spectacularly they were developing cotton textile mills, built almost entirely with Southern capital.

These mills employed whites only—usually poorer whites from the back country, whose lives had been one long experience of grinding poverty. Now they had steady jobs at what seemed to them good wages; and the cheap company housing supplied them was secure and comfortable compared to the ramshackle cabins to which they had been accustomed. While many of Charles Nordhoff's reports must be treated with caution, since they were based on native white testimony, there seems little reason to doubt his claim that the cotton mill workers were "evidently happy and pleased with their life." Their very satisfaction with their lot gave them a vested interest in white supremacy—it helped keep black labor out of the mills.

Further, Conservatives were active in promoting railroad expansion at a time when every Southern town and village was clamoring for railroad connections. Although they joined forces with Yankees in numerous projects, their influence was exercised most effectively through the Louisville and Nashville Railroad, a potent Conservative political and economic force not only in Kentucky and Tennessee but also in Louisiana, Alabama, and Georgia. The position of Conservatives as leaders in Southern economic progress was further enhanced by their active support of the transcontinental railroad promotions of Scott and Huntington.

Through such varied appeals, Conservatives rallied much of white opinion behind them. There remained the problem of weakening the Republican party—or more accurately, the individual state Republican parties—enough that Conservatives could take power. And the Republicans were vulnerable. As one Conservative put it, "We must spread our nets to get in all the disaffected of the Republican party, white and black, and they are not a few." Blacks and whites were united within it in uneasy alliance—a reality of which Conservatives took full advantage, as will be seen later.

Even within white ranks there were situations which allowed room for Conservative maneuver. In nearly every state there were Republican leaders, such as Rufus B. Bullock of Georgia, who were intimately associated in business enterprises with their political foes, as Bullock was with Charles J. Jenkins, who had been removed as governor for his active hostility to the Reconstruction acts. Such associations gave Republicans and Conservatives so involved a community of economic interest which transcended formal political lines.

There were also in the Republican leadership native whites, like Orr of South Carolina and Alcorn of Mississippi, who were basically Conservative in outlook—they differed with Conservatives not on ends but on means. Given proper circumstances, such men might be won over. And, if Conservatives had to placate Republican politicians in order to get favors, it was equally true that once the favors were granted, the Conservatives, through their business connections, were in a position to reward Republicans who strayed from party regularity.

Besides, for various reasons, including quarrels over the spoils of office and dispensation of favors to business rivals, the various state parties were divided into feuding factions. Conservatives in each state hoped to exploit the given situation to best advantage; in some they might obtain only a weakening of the Republicans, in others they might win power.

In states like South Carolina and Mississippi, where regular Republican rule appeared impregnable (thanks to the large bloc of black voters led by competent black men), Conservatives strove to divide the party by fanning the flames of intraparty dissension, and shrewdly allied themselves with movements that claimed to be "reform." This gave them an opportunity to exploit the corruption issue to the fullest. Thus, in South Carolina in 1872 they backed the "reform" Republican ticket sponsored by Orr. While this met with little response, similar backing to bolting Republicans two years later was successful enough to prompt some Conservatives to speculate on a decisive struggle in 1876.

In Mississippi, Conservatives threw their support to Alcorn when, in 1873, he tried to unseat his fellow Republican, Adelbert Ames. Little power was gained by such moves, but progress was made in splitting the Republicans—and in Mississippi, Conservatives drew off permanently from the Republicans many leading whites, both native and Northern.

In states where the black vote was weaker and lacked adequate leadership, Conservatives were better able to use Republican division to win power. In Virginia's first election under Reconstruction, Conservatives abandoned their own candidate for governor when the Republicans split, and supported Gilbert C. Walker, a former Northern Democrat who showed sympathy for the Conservative view. Walker's victory ushered in permanent Conservative control. In Arkansas rivalry between Republican factions became so bitter as to result in armed struggle, necessitating federal intervention. Conservatives in the state, themselves hitherto divided, now united and swept both Republican factions into the discard in 1874. Less bloody dissension characterized Texas Republicanism, but bitterness in 1873 was so intense as to permit Conservative victory.

This legitimate political activity of Conservatives might well have won their aims in itself, given the fragmentation of Republican parties and the trend in national affairs against federal intervention in Southern politics. A considerable number of native whites, however, were not content with the relatively slow method of winning control by purely peaceful means. To the maneuverings of the politicians they added violence.

The assertion of federal authority through the Ku Klux Klan law had brought about a decline in Southern violence, but the Democratic victories of 1874 and the evident reluctance of the Grant Administration to interfere in the South helped bring about a resurgence of terrorism. Floggings and killings were accompanied in some areas by rigid social ostracism of white Republicans. Mississippi was not the only state where local Conservatives could boast, as they did to Charles Nordhoff, that they had made it "too damned hot" for white Republicans.

Complete Conservative victory was impossible, however, so long as black voters remained faithful to the Republican party. There were at least 450,000 of them, overwhelmingly located in the South and concentrated in the three states which held out longest against Conservatism—South Carolina, Mississippi, and Louisiana. Beginning in 1868, when for the first time in American history black men voted in a national election, a major Conservative aim was to undermine this black political power.

In that election the Conservative approach can at best be described as naïve. They hopefully enlisted the aid of various "Uncle Toms" to persuade black men to vote for white men who were attacking them in the North. They also sought to impress Negroes with their incompetency and to warn them against perfidious white Republicans. Thus Benjamin H. Hill to Georgia Negroes:

> You well know your race is not prepared to vote. Why do you care to do what you do not understand? Improve yourselves, . . . live in peace with your neighbors and drive off, as you would a serpent, the miserable dirty adventurers who come among you, and who, being too low to be received into white society, seek to foment among you a hatred for the decent portion of the white race. . . .

Such approaches were later abandoned, but Conservatives also employed in 1868 methods later used with considerable effect. Employers threatened to—and in some cases did—discharge black workers who voted for Grant. Tenants and sharecroppers were warned that voting

Republican would result in eviction. Assassination of black and white Republicans was frequent; Governor Bullock of Georgia reported that his state was in a "reign of terror."

At the time, however, such methods, while they helped carry Louisiana and Georgia for Seymour, also had counter-productive aspects in the eyes of the "new men" coming to the fore as Conservative leaders. Black men, instead of being cowed, went to the polls in great numbers, helping to swell Grant's popular vote and bolstering Republican strength in Congress in face of mounting Democratic sentiment among white voters. The Southern violence contributed to unifying the fissured Northern Republicans and brought to their support the abolitionists, Northern Methodists aroused over attacks on their missionaries (including the murder of Benjamin F. Randolph, a Negro), and members of the Grand Army of the Republic. In addition to strengthening Republicans, terrorism scared off Northern capital and if persisted in, would surely invite federal intervention in the South, and thereby hinder realization of the Conservative program.

Such considerations had little place in the minds of Conservative followers. They wanted white supremacy immediately, regardless of the hazards. Their temper was expressed by a Mississippi editor: "This is a White Man's Government; and trusting in our firm purpose, our good right arms, and God of Right, we will maintain it so."

The problem for Conservative leaders was to provide enough leeway for such sentiment to express itself while restricting it sufficiently to avoid federal action. Symbolically, Nathan B. Forrest of Tennessee and John B. Gordon of Georgia were Klan leaders while they pursued more prosaic business interests. But, lacking a disciplined, centralized organization, Conservative strategy was at the mercy of the secret societies (the Klan having been formally dissolved in 1869) over which they had little control. The recurring waves of violence finally brought response. In 1871 Congress passed the Ku Klux Klan law, making terroristic activities federal offenses and investing the President with sweeping power to suppress them. Even the limited exercise of his authority by Grant was sufficient to cow the terrorists. Violence by no means disappeared, but the conspiratorial organizations lost the initiative—and this opened the way for Conservative leaders to employ more sophisticated means to undermine black political power.

The means included all the tricks of fraud and deception practiced by politicians in both North and South to take advantage of the poor and illiterate. More basically they involved application of the old rule: divide and conquer.

One aspect was the wooing of Negro voters and leaders to bring them into the Conservative camp. Benjamin H. Hill, who had told black men they were unfit to vote, now cultivated their votes, as did Wade Hampton in South Carolina. Conservatives had some success with well-to-do Negroes, such as Gilbert Myers of Mississippi, who identified their interests with those of the white majority, and with some artisans and mechanics who distrusted the clamor of other black men for equal rights. Conservatives even converted some Republicans, the most notable example being former United States Senator Hiram R. Revels of Mississippi. He campaigned actively for Conservatives in the bitter election of 1875, which turned the state over to Conservative control.

Most blacks remained unconvinced, but that gave more point to another feature of Conservative strategy: exploitation of black grievances within the Republican party, even to supporting black candidates who challenged the party organization.

How far Conservatives were willing to go is indicated by the confused and embittered 1872 campaign in Louisiana. Taking advantage of a badly fragmented Republican party, the Conservatives were instrumental in drawing up a "fusion" slate headed by John McEnery, a Conservative. The second place, as the candidate for lieutenant governor, went to a Negro, D. B. Penn, who had been nominated for governor by the Liberal Republicans after they bolted the regular party. (It may be noted that Penn took an active role in the armed uprising in New Orleans in 1874 which sought to impose the McEnery ticket by force.)

In that same year South Carolina Conservatives backed a "reform" Republican ticket which included Martin R. Delany, a black man of excellent educational background, who enjoyed considerable prestige among Negroes. Delany, running for lieutenant governor, even solicited Conservative backing! Mississippi Conservatives likewise supported a bolting Republican slate which included a little-known black politician. They also helped to stimulate a feud between the weak and venal black lieutenant governor, A. K. Davis, and the honest carpetbag governor, Adelbert Ames.

In its early stages the Conservative wooing of blacks was directed largely at drawing off votes from the regular Republicans. By the early 70's, however, it took on a new dimension by helping foment discord within the regular Republican party over distribution of public offices. From the beginning whites, both Yankee and Southern, had been reluctant to share office with blacks. Even in the states where blacks outnumbered whites, the acceptance of major black office-holders was largely token. The first Reconstruction governments in South Carolina and Mississippi, for example, included only one black man each, and each was Secretary of State: James D. Lynch in Mississippi and Francis L. Cardozo in South Carolina. Louisiana, perhaps because of its aggressive, wealthy Negro community in New Orleans, had two Negroes in its first government: Oscar J. Dunn, Lieutenant Governor, and Antoine Dubuclet, Treasurer.

Restriction of black office-holding reflected in part the white desire to monopolize public posts. It also was the result of a feeling by both white and black leaders that too much show of black men in high office would alienate white opinion, including that of native whites whom Republicans hoped to win over. While some militants rejected the rationale, conservative black opinion, represented in South Carolina by Delany and Cardozo and in Mississippi by Lynch and Revels, prevailed. Such men counselled ambitious Negroes to prove themselves in county and municipal posts, and "they may expect to attain to some others in time."

By the 70's many black politicians felt the time had come. The black vote was active, and, while still loyal to Republicanism, was restive under the party's failure to improve their lot, to say nothing of its inability to protect black life, property, or jobs. This mood provided a basis on which to challenge conservative black leaders. In challenging the conservative view, the discontented blacks pointed out that they had proved themselves as competent and as honest as white men in the offices open to them and that such offices were disproportionately few. John R. Lynch, black Congressman from Mississippi, later estimated that blacks held not more than 5 per cent of the local offices in his state. In South Carolina the proportion appears to have been much higher, but still far short of black expectations.

In that state the black campaign for office was surprisingly successful. Increasingly blacks won Republican nomination, and then election. In 1872, for example, loyally supporting the Grant slate, they substantially increased the number of elected black office-holders within the state; of the state's five Congressmen, four were now black! Black success, however, had its debits. Poorer native whites, often bitterly racist in view, deserted the Republicans. Many Northerners were alienated, their careers sacrificed to open the way for black men or to make place on the ticket for those whites the blacks preferred—members of old South Carolina families who had gone Republican. That this was understandable in view of the long-standing associations between such families and the black elite of Charleston and Columbia made it no more palatable to the displaced Yankees. Nor did the honest men among them relish being lumped together with crooked Northerners as plunderers and "birds of prey" in the speeches of some Negro leaders.

In Mississippi the situation was more explosive. Black pressure for office helped precipitate an exodus of white men from the Republican party in 1873. In the ensuing election contest the native white, Alcorn, received Conservative endorsement in his effort to wrest party control from Ames. In the campaign the issue of "Negro domination" played a significant part. Raising the race issue solidified the black vote: all three black nominees for high office were elected, and black representation in the legislature increased.

The very magnitude of black success contributed to Conservative strength. Stripped of so many white members, the Republican party could the more readily be pictured as the black man's party, the success of which threatened white society. The embittered bolters, frustrated in their ambitions, were willing to make common cause with Conservatives determined to overthrow Republican government and restore white supremacy. These elements played a part in the 1875 election in which Conservatives won control.

While Conservatives reaped such advantage as they could from black pressure for office, they also pressed the issue which proved so effective in dividing white Republicans—corruption. This posed perhaps an even more distressing problem to blacks than to whites, for black men realized that a successful struggle for equality rested in large measure on honest leadership. But, Southern blacks knew full well that under Greeley's banner of "Reform and Reunion" marched men bitterly hostile to black rights. They also knew that stepping along smartly with the reformers were men, such as Warmoth of Louisiana, who were synonymous with corruption. Dire indeed might be the fate of Southern black men should the "reformers" succeed. Nevertheless, corruption was there, blocking black advances in such fields as civil rights and education (diversion of public school funds, for example). How was the black voter to deal with this dilemma?

The dilemma presented itself in another way to black leaders of integrity, such as James D. Lynch of Mississippi and Francis L. Cardozo of South Carolina. If they bolted the regular party organization they reduced, and perhaps destroyed, their influence on the course of events; they weakened the one political body on which black hopes rested; and they played into the hands of men whose basic motives they distrusted. On the other hand, refusal to bolt meant continuing in office with white men whose venality was notorious, and however honest their own behavior might be, they would be smeared by the wide brush wielded by

Conservatives—a brush which had obvious racist streaks in it. Most leaders—and voters—solved the dilemma by remaining within the Republican party and working to reform it from within.

Congressman Alonzo J. Ransier stated their position clearly:

> I am no apologist for thieves; . . . Nor am I luke warm on the subject of better government in South Carolina . . . [but] such is the determined opposition to the Republican party . . . by our opponents that no administration of our affairs, however honest, just, and economical, would satisfy any considerable portion of the [Conservatives]. . . . [I am] satisfied that the principles and policy of the great Republican party . . . are best adapted for promotion of good government to all classes of men, . . .

Ransier called on his followers to actively engage in "the work of reform" and in party conventions to nominate only "men who are above suspicion." In this way the community as a whole would be "best protected and the equal rights of all guaranteed and made safe."

Such views, while widely held, were not universal. Some blacks believed the Republican party to be so hopelessly corrupt as to defy reform. Some ambitious men, frustrated by their opponents' control of party machinery, thought they could fare better in alliance with Conservatives as "reform" candidates. And a few objected to the control of blacks in the party by the black elite.

In South Carolina, R. H. King tried to organize a black reform movement based on "honest mechanics and farmers whose minds are not biased by chicanery." Martin R. Delany, while proclaiming his allegiance to the Republican party, broke with it in 1872 and again in 1874, when his ticket openly solicited Conservative backing. In Louisiana, D. B. Penn led a considerable number of blacks out of the regular party. Later, during the final stages of Reconstruction, the most prominent black politician in the state, Lieutenant Governor P. B. S. Pinchback, deserted to the Conservatives, claiming the Republican organization "too corrupt for me to stand by it any longer." This was part of the rationale offered by Hiram Revels in Mississippi when he too went over to the Conservatives.

In summary, the corruption issue, while not as effective with black as with white Republicans, did introduce doubt, distrust, and some real division in the black community.

Behind the Conservative strategy of weakening black power through political means lay the ultimate sanction of coercion. Dampened down after partial enforcement of the Ku Klux Klan law and by internal state considerations which argued against violence, terrorism came to the fore again after 1874. How many blacks were beaten, flogged, and murdered may never be known, but the violence was so widespread and has been so well documented, that review of the evidence seems superfluous. Some comments are in order, however.

While some of the violence was personal and indiscriminate, leading some white editors to call for a halt lest planters lose their labor supply, much of it was directed against black leadership at the grass-roots level. These were members of Republican clubs, churches, and other organizations, men who actively promoted racial solidarity and a sense of race pride. Obscure men, lost to history, they represented what whites feared greatly: growth of local leadership based on farmers, laborers, and sharecroppers, with all that implied for social and economic relationships in the rural areas where most Southerners lived. As John Childers, a black man from Alabama who had been "persuaded" to vote Conservative told a Congressional committee, white violence was specially aimed at "these men that contends [sic] for their equal rights for person and property with the white men."

Some of these blacks could be singled out by their prominence in parades and public meetings. Others were identified by black informers, men who for a variety of reasons wished to ingratiate themselves with whites. How much the killing off of local leadership contributed to the post-Reconstruction black submissiveness remains to be studied.

White hostility to black militancy was further demonstrated in the campaign against the Negro militias. These had been organized partly as a means to mobilize black political power in the interests of incumbent Republican regimes, partly in response to Negro demands for protection against the wave of white terrorism in the late 60's. The militias were open to all citizens, but few whites joined, while, for obvious reasons, black men enlisted in great numbers, including Union war veterans and young militants. White hostility quickly centered on them: it was held that the spectacle of black men parading and drilling with arms so enraged white people that new waves of violence erupted, bringing with them the danger of race war.

Thus was explained the attacks of armed white mobs, led by Klansmen, on militia companies in South Carolina during 1870–1871, which finally resulted in Republican Governor R. K. Scott disarming the blacks. White violence temporarily subsided, but renewed white violence eventually led to re-arming some black units. Whites retaliated with the notorious Hamburg massacre of 1876, when an armory,

located in a town inhabited almost entirely by Negroes, was bom-
barded with cannon, the militiamen driven out, and many slaughtered
after they had surrendered.

The rationale that black militias incited white violence was also used
during the 1875 election campaign in Mississippi. Appalled at the white
terrorism, Governor Ames began organizing militia units—but his ad-
visors, white and black, said such a move would result only in more
violence. Ames, deserted by the Grant Administration and presumably
reassured by Conservative pledges of non-violence (pledges which were
not kept, and probably could not have been kept in view of white opinion), yielded. Ames knew full well this assured Conservative victory,
but his words of justification provide revealing insight into what was
happening in his state: "let us be at peace and have no more killing."

Another aspect of the resort to violence requires comment. It has
been claimed that, in the final stages of Reconstruction, Conservatives
resorted less to actual force and relied more on a show of force to in-
timidate black voters. Thus, under the famed "Mississippi plan" of 1875,
copied a year later in South Carolina, armed white bands paraded openly,
sometimes with cannon, forced Republican meetings to allow Conservatives to speak, and in a variety of "peaceful" ways created fear among the
blacks. The show of force was effective because behind it was genuine
menace, as the experience of Republicans in Mississippi in 1875 showed
and the Hamburg massacre demonstrated in South Carolina.

The purpose of political terrorism was, of course, to break black
spirit. In this, the program apparently succeeded in Mississippi, although
it is not at all clear that it did so in South Carolina. It is of significance,
however, that while some blacks were cowed, others resisted. Many
militia companies fought stubbornly when attacked. Mass meetings of
Charleston Negroes denouncing the Hamburg "riot" heard demands
that any repetition be met with black reprisals. In the tense atmosphere
produced by the affair, a clash between black Republicans and white
Conservatives in Charleston resulted in a major riot, during which,
for a time, the center of the city was in Negro hands.

When whites in New Orleans raised armed rebellion in 1874 the
city police, made up largely of blacks, bore the brunt of the battles
which followed. The earlier massacre of blacks at Colfax, Louisiana,
grew out of black resistance to an overwhelming white force. Black
militants were especially bitter against blacks who went over to the
Conservatives. These were often assaulted, and their houses and barns
burned. There seems little evidence, however, of murder of black Conservatives for their political activities.

Resistance, however, met with little approval from either whites sympathetic to the Negro or from black leaders themselves. Their counsel was patience, lest black resistance inspire even more white violence. A telling argument was what white men were doing at that very time to resisting Indians in the West!

Force, and the show of force, were linked to economic pressure. Southern employers and planters, like Northern businessmen, expected as a matter of loyalty that employees should vote as their masters dictated. Black men who voted Republican suddenly found themselves out of work, or in the case of sharecroppers, driven off the land, usually without the formality of being paid their share of the crop. To make the punishment effective, Southerners used a device much favored by anti-union employers in the North: the blacklist. Circulation of names of "troublemakers" among employers and planters of a given area effectively barred the men from earning their livelihood. Thus men, already wretchedly poor, were driven to traveling long distances in order to secure employment.

There was nothing subtle or hidden about the operation. It appeared early in the first elections in Virginia under the Reconstruction acts. Negro iron miners who voted the regular Republican ticket were fired. Newspapers lauded the employers, exclaiming that such blacks should be the last to complain about their treatment. In every Southern election the pattern was repeated, and by 1876 one Mississippi editor even tried to persuade Negroes of the rightness of it all: "If you owned land and had tenants on it, who voted against you, whenever they had a chance, . . . wouldn't you want to get rid of them?" The attitude of the black press was typified in one editor's denunciation of the blacklist as designed "so that none but servile tools may have work, while *men* will be rejected and reduced to starvation"; he called for an end to the "proscription of men for belonging to a political organization."

Negroes tried to end the practice. A few, like Lewis Lindsay, a Virginian, urged violent retaliation, but most felt the solution must come through political action. Black legislators took the lead in attempting to outlaw economic terrorism—to no avail. State action failing, black conventions in various states appealed to Congress for aid, linking the violence of the secret societies with the economic warfare as part of a plan to destroy black political power.

The case was put in a memorial to Congress from Alabama Negroes in 1874 explaining how their civil and political rights were violated:

> The means used . . . have been various; but have chiefly consisted of violence . . . and by depriving or threatening to deprive us of

employment and the renting of lands, which many of us, in our poverty and distress, were unable to disregard. These acts of lawlessness have been repeated . . . since our first vote in 1868, and their effect has been such that from ten to fifteen thousand . . . votes of our race have in each election been either repressed or been given under compulsion to our political opponents.

In 1874 Congressional Republicans, on whom black hopes rested, were little inclined to heed black protests. The memorials were filed and forgotten. Even the vaunted Civil Rights Act of 1875 provided no protection for workers victimized because of their political opinions.

Coercion, then, combined with the splitting tactics employed by Conservatives, helped to undermine black power. These methods might not have proved so successful had it not been for a growing feeling among blacks that while the Republican party was their last, best hope, it was not to be depended on. The old abolitionist group, led by Stevens and Sumner, was weaker with every election; Stevens himself died in 1868 and Sumner in 1874. Now the party was dominated by practical men whose interest in black men extended only so far as to keep them in the party column.

True, the Ku Klux Klan law had proved beneficial, but much of the funds appropriated for enforcement went to battle Democratic machines in Northern cities. In the meantime, the Grant Administration showed decreasing interest in protecting black rights in the South. Negro conventions repeatedly called for a national civil rights act, but none was passed until 1875, under circumstances which showed more concern with the presidential election of 1876 than with civil rights. Even so, the measure as passed omitted a feature many blacks deemed basic—equal rights in education.

Nor did Republicans have any program to cope with the distress arising from the depression after 1873, except to let economic "nature" take its course—a prescription which condemned the mass of poor blacks to even direr poverty.

Some blacks saw the situation as hopeless and urged emigration to Africa. Henry M. Turner, later a bishop of the African Methodist Episcopal Church, whose speech on his expulsion from the Georgia legislature in 1868 we have already cited, was the most articulate spokesman for this view. It is significant that he was later joined by such practical politicians as Richard H. Cain and Martin R. Delany—both of whom, ironically, had sought Conservative support during their careers. In the case of Delany it marked revival of an old project. During the 1850's, in collaboration with the famed black Northern abolitionist and preacher, Henry Highland Garnet, he had carefully developed an African emigration scheme which, he hoped, would help bring about the collapse of slavery in the United States.

To most black leaders African colonization was a chimera. America, not Africa, was now the American black's homeland, they held, and they looked for solution of their problems through American institutions. While some held firm to the belief that the Republican party was *the* institution through which black aspirations would be realized, increasing numbers of black leaders came to believe that this attitude in itself hindered realization of black hopes. So long as white Republicans could take the black vote for granted they need make few concessions to it. The answer was to demonstrate that black men could be politically independent. Thus, in 1872, while some blacks deserted to the Liberal Republicans in hope of furthering their careers, others, such as the noted black abolitionist and educator, Peter H. Clark of Cincinnati, did so because they wished to demonstrate political independence. Such a demonstration, they hoped, would not only improve black bargaining power but also aid in breaking down white prejudice.

By 1874 disenchantment with the Republican party had reached a point where it was possible for prestigious black leaders to suggest that there was some virtue in the Democrats. William Still, a prominent Northern black who had been active in the Underground Railroad, conceded that it was impossible for Negroes to vote Democratic at the moment, but he counselled his fellows against "wholesale denunciation of every Democrat." Many Democrats, he said, no longer held the prewar views of their party, "and while they still hold on to their party they are anxious for a general change, in which the civil and political rights of the colored man shall be recognized."

Black doubts about the Republican party reflected a correct reading of the political barometer. Pressures within the Republican party were forcing it further and further away from commitment to black men. As we have seen, Reconstruction policy, while it owed much to abolitionists, was more basically expression of fear that unity of the white South and Northern Democrats would imperil Republican policy in such matters as the national debt, the tariff, the national banking system, and federal subsidies to railroads.

So long as the fear persisted, black rights were safe. When it dissipated, the black man was in trouble, for there was no strong body of white opinion in the North to sustain black men's rights.

Northern fears began to dissipate when the Southern "new men" came to the fore—they talked the same language as Northern business-

men. They offered no threat to the payment of the national debt. Coal
and iron operators of Tennessee and Alabama were as anxious for tariff
protection as those of Pennsylvania. Their complaints about the national banking system was not that it was bad but that the South
shared too little in it. Far from being opposed to railroad subsidies,
Southerners fought for them, even against Northern Democratic opposition. They saw eye-to-eye with Northern business on keeping labor,
white as well as black, "in its place." Eager for Northern capital, they
worked loyally with it.

To capitalists timid about going into a region where neither life nor
property seemed safe, they gave assurances, backed by such examples
as Virginia, that with Conservatives in control, law and order were
restored. All of this was done, too, Conservatives assured Northerners,
without violating any basic rights of black men. Were not black men
still serving in the legislatures under Conservative control? Were there
not black men who supported the Conservative cause?

Many Northern Republicans were willing to be convinced. Southern
Conservatives presented no menace to vital Northern interests, and they
were pledged to respect the rights of black men. Some otherwise practical politicians argued that on this basis the old national Whig Party
could be reconstituted, made up of Northern Republicans and Southern
Conservatives, who were Republican in everything but name. Such a
party, in context of the social upheavals threatened by the Panic of
1873, would provide a bulwark of property rights against the malcontent
Grangers of the prairies and the socialist appeals to hungry workmen
in the cities. In short, the basic interests of the Republican party lay
in alliance with Southern Conservatives, not with Southern blacks.

Whatever doubts may have lingered in Northern minds were dissipated by 1874. Conservatives *were* winning control in Southern states,
and therefore had to be dealt with; and in their control there was not
much for Northern businessmen to dislike. Peace was restored. Taxes
were reduced—and if that meant in some cases that Southern youngsters went without schooling, what concern was that of the Yankee?

Conservative governments were perhaps even friendlier to business
than Republican—their leaders were thoroughly imbued with a business
point of view. Conservatives helped mobilize support for the Texas
and Pacific project. The man who tried to drive it through Congress
was L. Q. C. Lamar, who symbolized the appeal of the "new men" to
Northern business by simultaneously trying to get federal subsidies for
a Northern project, the Northern Pacific Railroad. It is significant that
Lamar was frustrated not by Republicans, but by Northern Democrats.

The final indication of working cooperation between Southern Conservatives and Northern Republicans came in the disputed election of 1876. In the tortuous, secret negotiations and in the acrimonious debates which accompanied the vote count, Southern Conservatives deserted Northern Democrats to assure Rutherford B. Hayes peaceful assumption of the Presidency.

All this involved bargaining. The Conservative price, in part, was withdrawal of national Republican support from the three remaining Republican governments in the South and recognition of their Conservative rivals. Republicans paid, in full knowledge that implicit in the bargain was something of great import: henceforth the fate of the black man in the South would be in the hands of native whites. Some Republicans had uneasy consciences, to judge from the frequent assurances from Hayes and others that the black man would be better off with people who "understood" him than with federal protection.

Besides, such men had pledges from Conservatives that black rights would be respected. Wade Hampton, the new Governor of South Carolina, bespoke the formal Conservative position in assuring that his administration stood by its pledge that citizens of both races and parties would "be regarded as equals in the eyes of the law—all to be fully protected in the enjoyment of every political right now possessed by them."

Scant attention was paid to complaints of Southern Republicans that men like Hampton made "fine speeches" for national consumption while conniving at violence against black and white Republicans. As Pierrepont had said earlier, Northerners—businessmen, farmers, workers—were "tired" of these everlasting complaints.

So, Hayes took office peacefully. It was indicative of things to come that when he visited Richmond, Virginia, shortly after his inauguration, the city was "prettied up" for him by black men in chain gangs.

CHAPTER **7**

Equality—
A National Commitment?

How is Reconstruction to be appraised in terms of its significance to American black men?

Fundamentally, it represented the first major test of black belief that white Americans would honor the national commitment to equality set forth in the Declaration of Independence and applied specifically to black men in the Reconstruction amendments. Black men, for the most part, believed they could successfully integrate themselves into American life as equals. In so doing they would also solve the problem of identity by demonstrating that above all they were Americans. This note was struck at the founding convention of the National Equal Rights League: "Here were we born, for this country our fathers and brothers fought, and here we hope to remain in the full enjoyment of enfranchised manhood."

Belief in integration called for active participation in American life. As we have seen, to a degree unparalleled in American history—and in the annals of white nations generally—black men voted and held public office. Thanks in large part to their efforts Southern political life was democratized and infused with a social content to an extent hitherto unknown in Southern experience. Black children—and adults —swarmed into the schools, and many went on to the normal schools, colleges, and universities opened to them by Reconstruction governments. This, in turn, helped to swell the ranks of the miniscule black middle class of doctors, lawyers, merchants, and teachers. Black craftsmen and professional men sought, unsuccessfully, to identify themselves with their white counterparts.

The mass of blacks labored on construction gangs, in workshops, on fields and plantations, hoping to ameliorate their lot through economic and political action. A small number of them were able to acquire their

158

own land; a very few, exemplified by Senator Bruce of Mississippi, became wealthy.

This was an impressive record for a people only a few years away from slavery. The fact that it had been made in the face of white hostility gave black men confidence in their abilities and helped nourish a sense of black worth and dignity. Indeed, they could hope that they were in process of overcoming white prejudice. Did not Pollard's essay augur a shift in Southern white attitudes? Black men could feel that through their contributions they were helping to make the experiment in integration a success.

Dominant though the sentiment for integration may have been, there were also within the black community strong currents of separatism, deriving from various sources. One source was the deep psychological need of black people to nurture their own institutions and direct their own affairs, to have some place of their own where they could be their own selves. Thus, the rapid development of the Negro church. Another source was the rejection of blacks by white society. The color line was drawn in social life, in the workshops and professions, and eventually in politics. Black men, perforce, were compelled to organize their own unions and professional associations and to develop a social life of their own.

This does not imply that such separatism was opposed to the goal of integration: black churchmen, union members, and professional men were in general as dedicated to that goal as others. Integration, they believed, did not preclude the existence of black institutions such as the Negro church. Secular organizations arose not out of black desire for separation but from white hostility.

Some, like Henry M. Turner, were separatists on principle. Disillusioned with white men and white policies, they held America had little to offer black men save subordination. To them, there was only one way out, the ultimate in separatism—return to Africa, the black homeland. Black identity was not with America, but with Africa.

Such a view was unacceptable to the mass of blacks, who, making progress, slow though it may have been, believed the goal of integration to be realistic. As it turned out, their faith proved to be unrealistic. Why?

It must be recalled that the basic problem confronting the nation after the war was the place of the black man in American society. The Thirteenth Amendment made him free. Was he also a citizen? The Fourteenth Amendment declared that he was. Was he a full citizen, with rights and responsibilities equal to those of white men? The Fifteenth

Amendment and the supporting body of Reconstruction legislation answered in the affirmative.

Yet Reconstruction was fundamentally a white man's policy. To be sure, state and national conventions of black men had repeatedly demanded citizenship and the ballot, but no black men sat in the Congress which shaped the basic laws. Black men, in later Congresses, backed legislation promoting black rights, but passage of such laws was conditioned upon white interests, and their enforcement and interpretation were entirely in white hands.

There were whites and whites, of course. Some, like Stevens and Sumner, had a genuine interest in black welfare as such. Most white politicians were concerned rather with how black political power could be used to subdue still rebellious Southern whites and to serve the mundane interests embraced within the Republican party. Such were the exigencies of the moment that these ends could best be served by extending citizenship and the ballot to blacks. Then, to implement this policy, Republicans were impelled by the logic of events, especially by developments in the South, to promote black rights in fields other than politics.

On such pragmatic basis America met the issue of the place of the black man in its society: expediency forced assertion of principle—but we must not lose sight of the fact that the principle enunciated was equality.

White opinion, however, while willing to tolerate the formal principle, was not prepared to accept it in practice. Expediency thus dictated masking the principle, even to the point of its tacit disavowal, as when Republicans sold the Reconstruction policy to Northern voters by appealing to racist fears. In the South, where such an approach was impractical, application of the principle was vitiated from the beginning by failure to give land to the freedmen. In neither section was much effort made, except by individual teachers and preachers, such as Wendell Phillips and Gilbert Haven, to persuade whites that Reconstruction presented opportunity for a great experiment in shaping a bi-racial society of free and equal Americans. This in turn derived from the failure of white leadership to envision Reconstruction in such terms.

It followed, then, that whites assumed that while black men were free and were citizens they were also "naturally" inferior and thus would accept subordinate status. When it became clear that black men not only sought equality, but were attaining it in such visible areas as public office, white fears of black men revived. Northerners, disabused of their fears of black hordes pouring across the Ohio river, were the more ready to believe Southern Conservatives that equality meant black oppression of whites. Whites in all sections were convinced that behind the demand for equality lurked a desire for racial amalgamation—and their ears were walls to all black arguments to the contrary. Thus, support for Reconstruction waned, and after the collapse of 1873 Northerners, preoccupied with their own problems, were content to let white men run the South in their own way.

Without at least the tacit acquiescence of Northern whites, it is difficult to believe that Northern business and its political associates could have gone as far as they did in accommodating Southern Conservatives. In this, as in other Reconstruction developments, the black man did not hold the initiative. No matter how much progress he might make, the black man's fate was still in white hands.

Another factor in the frustration of black hope for integration was that its attainment involved basic changes in American society which Americans were not prepared to make. Those abolitionists who entertained notions of equality after emancipation thought of it, for the most part, in terms of legal equality and equality of opportunity. They sought to help the black make the most of it by providing the rudiments of education and inculcating the puritan virtues of industry, thrift, frugality, sobriety, and self-discipline. Men so trained and so self-disciplined, it was believed, would in time acquire property and become respected members of their communities. Full equality would follow as a matter of course.

Some few, Thaddeus Stevens and Thomas Wentworth Higginson among them, thought this inadequate and unrealistic. It assumed that, given emancipation, Southern society would be an open society, when in fact it was a closed society, so far as the black man was concerned. It ignored the reality that no matter how good a man's character might be, if he lacked land, capital, and the knowledge of how to use them, he was at the mercy of those who did have them. And there was no denying that the mass of black men lacked all three.

If freedom were to be meaningful and equality assured, then the federal government must assume physical protection of the black man, promote his welfare, and underwrite his independence by land distribution. One method to attain these ends was represented in the Freedmen's Bureau; another was the proposal to provide land through confiscation of Confederate estates.

When these were raised as practical political issues it became clear that forces other than race feeling stood in the way of such a program for racial equality. Men on both sides of the issues perceived, however dimly, that their adoption entailed the remaking of American society.

For purely pragmatic reasons Congress in 1866 extended the life of the Freedmen's Bureau and added to its functions.

That the execution of these functions left much to be desired should not obscure the fact that the bureau represented something new in American life. As Andrew Johnson pointed out in his veto message of 1866, the bureau was unprecedented: it not only cut across traditional federal-state relationships, it was also a step in the direction of a welfare state, if we may paraphrase his words in today's terminology. As such it was as distasteful to many Northerners as it was to the President—one factor which contributed to its short lease of life.

The proposal for land confiscation touched an extremely sensitive point—the sanctity of private property. Northern leaders, having already "confiscated" more than a billion dollars of private property through emancipation, were little inclined to provide still another example for agrarian reformers and socialist spokesmen in the cities.

It was clear also that land distribution could be only a first step. Since black men lacked capital to work the land, it would have to be furnished. Two sources were open: private and public. If private, then the Federal Government, to protect the black man from usury, must oversee the transactions, just as it supervised labor contracts under the Freedmen's Bureau. If public, then government, federal or state, must regulate its use. From another angle, if the Stevens proposal to create a body of independent black yeomanry were adopted, this might well mean restriction of the black man's right to dispose of his own property —a principle dangerous to all private property. All of these possibilities represented, as did the Freedmen's Bureau, a turning away from free enterprise in the direction of social control.

White America was no more ready for such a step than any Western European nation. It was not simply a matter of race. It was also a matter of ideology and principle. This was the heyday of almost religious belief in the efficacy of the "hidden hand" of self-interest in bringing about social well-being, intensified by faith in the survival of the fittest as the test of social evolution. Both reinforced the inherited puritan teachings of the individual's responsibility for his well-being, spiritual and material. If an individual fell by the wayside, it was basically due to his own weaknesses, not to social ills. Thus was ruled out governmental intervention on behalf of the poor, white or black. It helps explain why Reconstruction lacked social content.

General acceptance of the social philosophy of *laissez-faire* meant distress for poor people generally. For propertyless blacks, subject to racial animosity, it was well-nigh disastrous. When the hope of land distribution proved illusory, they were at the mercy of a "free" labor market dominated by planters and employers. In that market there was little hope for progress, for equality.

The tragedy of black leadership was that it failed to perceive this. It, too, believed in *laissez-faire*. The educated elite, who set the tone for other black leaders, were products of colleges and universities, either in the North or abroad, which produced white elites. Like the whites, blacks accepted the teachings of Adam Smith as social and economic law. They, too, shared in the Puritan ethic of work as the way to moral and material well-being—and the individual's responsibility for both. Besides, few had experienced slavery, and while they knew white racism at first hand, they were only a little more sensitive than whites to the deep psychic scars left on a people by the "peculiar institution."

Among those who had been slaves, there were a few, such as Senator Bruce of Mississippi, who had gone on to become wealthy. It was easy for such self-made men to assume that because they had succeeded, others could also, providing they possessed the necessary character, shrewdness, and fortitude.

Time and again spokesmen for the elite insisted that all the black man needed was the right "to stand on his own feet." As Congressman Richard H. Cain of South Carolina put it: "Let the laws of the country be just; . . . that is all we ask. . . . Place all citizens upon one broad platform; and if the Negro is not qualified to hoe his row in this contest of life, then let him go down." Like white friends of the black man who shared similar views, Cain revealed an ignorance of the realities of life among the Negro masses—and displayed the gulf that yawned between the elite and the masses.

Both sought equality, but while the elite emphasized civil and political rights, the masses interpreted it in economic terms. They wanted land of their own—and they looked to government to provide it. Given their poverty and the conditions of Southern society they knew they had small chance of acquiring it on their own. In this context, *laissez-faire* was an impediment to realization of black hope. But black leaders also failed to see that *laissez-faire* in itself was inimical to all black aspirations.

Why? Because, with its exaltation of unrestricted individualism, it was in practice antisocial, tending to atomize and disintegrate society. Western societies in the nineteenth century responded to the danger by reinforcing the appeal of traditional religion with the newer sanctions of nationalism to provide a viable social system which transcended naked self-interest.

There was another aspect of *laissez-faire* which gradually became apparent to European workers: atomization of society served the interests of men who dominated the swiftly growing empire of industry and finance, men who rarely permitted specific differences to interfere with their common interest in maintaining the social and economic order from which they benefited. The workers' major responses were various forms of socialism and anarchism. Such ideologies asserted the worth and dignity of the common man, and so went far in helping develop a positive sense of identity and community among degraded people. They explained existing predicaments, not in terms of personal character, but as the result of impersonal social forces. The direction of these social forces could be changed by united collective action, consciously undertaken by their victims. As a result of such action, mankind as a whole would see a better world, freed from poverty, exploitation, and war. In other words, the ideologies furnished for people an explanation of their plight, absolved them of guilt for it, and offered solutions, based on conscious, united, positive action.

Such a unifying influence was lacking among blacks; all they had in common was their color, and that was not enough. Victims of a *laissez-faire* system in which their leaders believed, blacks were fragmented, and thus unable to confront successfully the Conservative-Republican coalition which effectively destroyed black political power and frustrated the black hope for integration into American society on the basis of equality.

The impact on black attitudes of what T. Thomas Fortune, the noted black editor, called the "betrayal" of 1876, cannot be overestimated. If it signalled the end of the hope for integration, it likewise marked the latest in what blacks considered to be a series of broken white pledges, beginning with the failure to grant land. It also ushered in a period when even the goal of equality receded into the distance, although it was never lost sight of.

True, for a generation after 1876 black men voted, held public office, and sat in Congress—but in ever diminishing numbers and on terms reflecting an understanding between such blacks and Southern Conservatives. For a time there was some respect for black civil rights. What remained of those, as well as of black political rights, were consumed in the flames of the political warfare of the 90's, when white Bourbons and white Populists fought for control of the South. No matter which side won, the black man lost. In state after state his degradation was written into law—and approved by the United States Supreme Court.

Nor was there much room for black men in the protest movements of the day. Populism attracted large numbers of black farmers until the white Populists turned on them. A few Negroes turned socialist, but the party was little interested in blacks as such. Many of the leaders were openly racist, and even Eugene V. Debs, who sympathized deeply with black men, thought they had no problems substantially different from those of white workers. The American Federation of Labor practiced segregation and its leaders were increasingly racist in public utterances.

Black hope for integration had proved unrealistic. Reality was the emergence of a color-caste system imbedded in the laws, behavior and attitudes of white America.

How did black men respond to this thwarting of their hope?

To some, the answer was separatism. Turner's project for a return to Africa took on a new lease of life; in 1886 an association formed for that purpose appealed to Congress for funds to help blacks emigrate. Others sought escape within the United States. In 1879, under conditions of incredible hardship, thousands fled the South for the prairies of Kansas in the first mass migration organized and directed by black men. There they hoped, vainly, to find the security and opportunity denied them in the South. Later, some blacks advocated migration to the Oklahoma territory, where they proposed to establish a separate Negro state. The fact that none of these projects was successful should not blind us to the fact that they represented among blacks a deep sense of rejection by white society.

Other blacks, equally sensitive to the decline in black fortunes, warned that giving way to counsels of despair was fatal. The proper answer, they said, was not withdrawal, but militancy. Thus, Frederick Douglass, in 1883, after the Supreme Court had struck down the Civil Rights Act of 1875:

> If the six million of colored people of this country, . . . have not sufficient spirit and wisdom to organize . . . to defend themselves from outrage, discrimination and oppression, it will be idle for them to expect that the Republican party or any other political party will . . . care what becomes of them. . . . we are men and must speak for ourselves, or we shall not be spoken for at all. . . .

Even more militant was T. Thomas Fortune, who, in 1884, advocated the unity of black and white poor to end the economic system which impoverished them. Hopefully he predicted: "When the issue is properly joined, the rich, be they black or be they white, will be found upon the same side; and the poor [black and white] will be found on the same side."

There were still other leaders who felt that political activity was futile and that emphasis should be placed on self-help: the development of character, morality, and race pride through black economic activity. One such approach was that of Alexander Crummell, a famous Episcopalian priest who formulated an early version of black nationalism; another was that of Booker T. Washington.

Crummell exhorted his fellows to cease depending on white men and to develop their own business enterprises, employing black capital and black labor, in both industry and agriculture. Such cooperation, he thought, would forge racial solidarity, stimulate a sense of black pride, develop black character, and eventually win recognition of black equality from whites. Washington denied that blacks could attain their goals without "a certain extent" of white cooperation. But he, too, laid emphasis on the need for blacks to develop their own resources, material, moral, and intellectual. Through such development blacks would win respect for their rights: "Brains, property, and character for the Negro will settle the question of civil rights," he said in 1884.

The last type of self-help appealed strongly to the emerging black bourgeoisie. Identifying themselves with white middle class values, they strove to prove themselves worthy of white acceptance. But always there was the color line. The response of many such blacks was particularly destructive to black psychological wholeness: they blamed the color line not on whites, but on the mass of blacks, who by their presumed vulgarity, laziness, thriftlessness, and immorality held back decent and industrious blacks from achieving their due. Bound to the black mass by color and by economic necessity, they psychologically rejected their fellows. Thus, they provided no leadership, and by the same token, the masses expected none from them.

As for the masses, their reaction to the collapse of black hope was withdrawal: they were in American society, but not of it. They adjusted themselves to the ways of white supremacy through a subtle and complex code of behavior toward whites which satisfied white men while it enabled black men to keep a measure of self-respect. The tensions inherent in such a delicate situation were eased in the outlets of revivalistic religion and in development of black standards of behavior within the black community—the standards which so offended middle class blacks. With the withdrawal, however, there came all too often acceptance of the notion that the mass of black men *were* inferior. White men "proved" it to them daily; successful black men said, in effect, that white men were right!

Not all successful black men, however. There were always leaders who held firm to the goal of equality, men who perceived the significance of Reconstruction policy as a white commitment to that goal.

We are apt to forget that, given the overwhelming white sentiment of the time, it is conceivable that while the Negro was given freedom he might also have been legally confined to subordinate status—as indeed he was under state legislation late in the century. Howell Cobb, the Georgia planter, argued for just such status as a substitute for slavery, and his ideas were echoed in the North by such prominent men as Senator Thomas A. Hendricks of Indiana and Francis P. Blair, who had been a staunch Unionist in Missouri during the war. Even among blacks there was some willingness in the immediate post-war period to accept subordination. A few state conventions hailed freedom as providing blacks the opportunity to demonstrate their potentialities but avoided calling for civil and political rights.

Whatever the motives of those who finally carried the day, a historically significant fact is that in its Reconstruction policy the nation, however reluctantly, opted for equality. This was no mean achievement. No other white people dealing with men of other color had so committed itself.

That whites did not live up to this commitment is abundantly plain. It is equally plain that while many of the Negro masses sank into passivity, many black leaders never ceased reminding whites of the broken pledge. Such spokesmen, ranging from the aging Douglass to the youthful DuBois, stirred white America's conscience with increasing effect. It is significant that prominent among the demands of the Niagara Movement, the organization of young black militants in the early years of this century, were those for enforcement of the Reconstruction amendments. The commitment recalled provided stimulus for the new white abolitionist response to the lynchings and race riots which scarred the nation's history at the turn of the century. Its embodiment in constitutional form and in legislation helped black men later, in the context of a changing world and changing American society, to bring forth from courts, legislatures, and Congress the civil rights decisions and legislation with which we are familiar. That long struggle, with its numerous setbacks and many successes, helped develop in black Americans renewed feelings of pride and dignity and a mounting sense of unity.

Reconstruction, then, to the black man was only a beginning. It was a faltering, but decisive, step from formal freedom to meaningful freedom, based on the civil and political equality of black men. The means necessary to provide a firm economic foundation for such equality— land for the farmer and workshops open to the craftsman—were denied,

Selected Bibliography

APTHEKER, HERBERT, ed., *A Documentary History of the Negro People in the United States*, Vol. II. New York: Citadel Press, 1951. Contains much material of value relating to Reconstruction.

BROCK, W. R., *An American Crisis: Congress and Reconstruction, 1865–1867*. London: St. Martin's Press, 1962. New look at Reconstruction by a British scholar.

BRODIE, FAWN M., *Thaddeus Stevens: Scourge of the South*. New York: W. W. Norton & Company, Inc., 1959. Comprehensive, sympathetic account of leading Reconstruction figure.

CONWAY, ALAN, *The Reconstruction of Georgia*. Minneapolis: University of Minnesota Press, 1966. State study by a British scholar.

COULTER, E. MERTON, *The South During Reconstruction, 1865–1877*. Baton Rouge: Louisiana State University Press, 1947. Interpretation markedly different from that of this work.

COX, LAWANDA, and JOHN H., *Politics, Principles and Prejudice, 1865–1866*. New York: The Free Press, 1963. Fresh study of the origins of Reconstruction policy.

CURRENT, RICHARD, ed., *Reconstruction, 1865–1877*. Englewood Cliffs, N.J.: Prentice-Hall, Inc., 1965. Valuable collection of original source readings.

DONALD, DAVID, *The Politics of Reconstruction, 1863–1867*. Baton Rouge: Louisiana State University Press, 1965. Presents much new material on complexities of Reconstruction politics.

DuBOIS, W. E. B., *Black Reconstruction in America, 1860–1880*. Cleveland: World Publishing Company, 1964. Paperback reprint of pioneer work of the black scholar who challenged older interpretations.

————, *The Souls of Black Folk*. New York: Fawcett Publications, 1961. Paperback reprint of a classic with much material relating to Reconstruction.

FRANKLIN, JOHN HOPE, *Reconstruction After the Civil War*. Chicago: University of Chicago Press, 1961. Survey of the post-war period by a leading Negro historian.

GOSSETT, THOMAS F., *Race: The History of an Idea in America*. Dallas: Southern Methodist University Press, 1963. Opening chapters indispensable for understanding racial theories and attitudes dominant in nineteenth century.

JORDAN, WINTHROP D., *White Over Black*. Chapel Hill: University of North Carolina Press, 1968. An excellent source for study of the origins and development of white attitudes toward blacks in the United States.

LYND, STAUGHTON, ed., *Reconstruction*. New York: Harper & Row, Publishers, 1967. Brief collection of differing interpretations.

McKITRICK, ERIC L., *Andrew Johnson and Reconstruction*. Chicago: University of Chicago Press, 1960. Detailed study of political infighting which brought about Congressional Reconstruction.

McPHERSON, JAMES M., *The Struggle for Liberty: Abolitionists and the Negro in the Civil War and Reconstruction*. Princeton, N.J.: Princeton University Press, 1964. Scholarly study of problems faced by abolitionists when confronted by black men as persons.

MEIER, AUGUST, *Negro Thought in America, 1880–1915*. Ann Arbor: University of Michigan Press, 1963. A pioneer study by a young scholar, rich in material and insights, with some valuable reflections on the Reconstruction period.

PATRICK, REMBERT W., *The Reconstruction of the Nation*. New York: Oxford University Press, Inc., 1967. Comprehensive survey of national as well as Southern developments.

QUARLES, BENJAMIN, *Frederick Douglass*. Englewood Cliffs, N.J.: Prentice-Hall, Inc., 1968. Combination of readings from Douglass together with commentary from men of his own time and present-day historical scholars.

RANDALL, J. G., and DAVID DONALD, *The Civil War and Reconstruction*, 2nd edition. Boston: D. C. Heath & Company, 1961. Updated edition of a standard work which interprets Reconstruction in light of recent scholarship.

ROSE, WILLIE LEE, *Rehearsal for Reconstruction: The Port Royal Experiment*. New York: Vintage Books, 1967. Paperback edition of well written account of how abolitionists during the Civil War proved that freedom for black men would work.

SINGLETARY, OTIS A., *Negro Militia and Reconstruction*. Austin: Texas University Press, 1957. Study of a much-neglected aspect of Reconstruction.

STAMPP, KENNETH M., *The Era of Reconstruction, 1865–1877*. New York: Alfred A. Knopf, Inc., 1965. Vigorous reinterpretation of the era in view of recent scholarly findings.

WHARTON, VERNON LANE, *The Negro in Mississippi, 1865–1890*. New York: Harper & Row, Publishers, 1965. Paperback reprint of a classic in its field.

WILLIAMSON, JOEL, *After Slavery: The Negro in South Carolina During Reconstruction, 1861–1877*. Chapel Hill: University of North Carolina Press, 1965. Valuable study of the complexities of white and black relationships in a single state.

WISH, HARVEY, ed., *The Negro Since Emancipation*. Englewood Cliffs, N.J.: Prentice-Hall, Inc., 1964. Documents that provide insight into black thinking.

———, *Reconstruction in the South, 1865–1877*. New York: Farrar, Straus & Giroux, Inc., 1965. Original source readings.

WOODWARD, C. VANN, *Origins of the New South, 1877–1913*. Baton Rouge: Louisiana State University Press, 1951. Opening chapters provide significant material on Reconstruction.

———, *Reunion and Reaction: The Compromise of 1877 and the End of Reconstruction*. New York: Doubleday Anchor Books, 1956. Paperback edition of a basic reinterpretation of ending of Reconstruction.

Index

173

ACKNOWLEDGEMENTS

Kumari Jayawardena greatly influenced the direction this book followed. It is thus fitting that the acknowledgements begin with her. Her unpublished research on the Women's Franchise Union and early feminism in Sri Lanka – which she so generously shared with me – inspired the character of Annalukshmi. Her books, *The Rise of the Labour Movement in Ceylon* and *The White Woman's Other Burden*, were also invaluable. Her stories about various Cinnamon Gardens families helped me get a sense of what went on beneath the polished veneer.

My gratitude to my partner, Andrew Champion, for his enormous patience with my daily doubts; his help with various knots in the plot; coming up with the title; martinis at six o'clock; good sense, plants, cats.

My thanks to my family, as always, for their support and love.

The following people read the early drafts of this novel and I am indebted to them for their valuable input: Rishika Williams and Fernando Sa-Pereira, who helped me with interesting insights into Annalukshmi's and Balendran's characters; also

Sunila Abeysekera, Manel Fonseka, Kumari Jayawardena, Jeff Round, Tony Stephenson.

I would like to give special thanks to my editor Ellen Seligman at McClelland & Stewart for her meticulous and creative editing of this book, for forcing me to go that extra mile (and for her strong faith that I could, indeed, do it); my editor Will Schwalbe at Hyperion in New York, for pointing out that a historical novel can be a metaphor for the present, for his encouraging calls and e-mails while I was in Sri Lanka, for his conviction that I could do it again; John Saddler at Anchor; my agents Bruce Westwood and Jennifer Barclay for, among other things, the box of books they sent me while I was in Sri Lanka – further proof that their regard for me goes beyond their excellent representation of my work internationally; Heather Sangster, formerly of McClelland & Stewart, who stuck with the copyediting even after she had left; Anne Valeri, my publicist at McClelland & Stewart.

This book was heavily reliant on research, so I wish to thank the following people for their time and effort: *In Sri Lanka*: Manel Fonseka, who put me into contact with numerous interesting people; Mr. C. I. Edwards, Sr., who, despite difficulties of speech because of illness, brought the 1920s alive for me; Reverend Lionel Peiries, for interesting reflections on the Cinnamon Gardens crowd; Mrs. Sathasivam of Cambridge Place, for details of Hindu culture and for arranging for me to visit a temple and its trustee; Chloe De Soysa, whose memories of the saris and food at her parents' parties provided helpful detail; Siro Gopallawa, who so patiently photocopied the Donoughmore Commission Report for me, five pages a day; Anjalendran, for help with architectural details; Jan Bruinsma, whose house was a haven for us during the year in Sri Lanka. *In Singapore and Malaysia:*

For the oral histories they shared with me – Dr. S. R. Sayampanathan, Mrs. Jayalukshmi Sivarajah of Klang, Dulcie Abraham, Mrs. Ampalapillai of Scotts Road. Mrs. Shellatay Rao of the Arkrib Negara and Dr. Kathirithamby-Wells pointed me in the right direction in terms of my research. Kurt Crocker and Andreas Wan for their hospitality. Ian Gomez for his friendship and good times, so essential when one is in a foreign country.

Other books were extremely helpful: K. M. De Silva's *A History of Sri Lanka*; S. W. R. D. Bandaranaike's *The Handbook of the Ceylon National Congress 1919-1928*; H. W. Cave's *The Book of Ceylon*; M. D. Raghavan's *Tamil Culture in Ceylon*; S. Namasivayam's *The Legislatures of Ceylon*; Rajakrishnan's *The Tamils of Sri Lankan Origin in the History of West Malaysia*, and Jeffrey Weeks' *Coming Out: Homosexual Politics in Britain from the Nineteenth Century to the Present*. The *Daily News* from 1927 and 1928 was an excellent source for period details, accounts of labour strikes and the Donoughmore hearings.

The photograph of a street in Cinnamon Gardens, which appears on the jacket of this book, is from H. W. Cave's *The Book of Ceylon* and was kindly re-photographed for me by Dominic Sansoni. The two people on the `jacket are, of course, real, and I am very grateful to their families for letting me use these photographs. The lives of these two people, however, in no way bear any resemblance to the lives of the characters in this book.

Sari Ginsberg

Shyam Selvadurai was born in 1965 in Colombo, Sri Lanka. He came to Canada with his family at the age of nineteen. He has studied creative writing and theatre, and has a B.F.A. from York University.

Funny Boy, his first novel, was published to immediate acclaim in 1994, was a national bestseller, and won the W.H. Smith/Books in Canada First Novel Award and, in the U.S., The Lambda Literary Award, and was named a Notable Book by the American Library Association. *Cinnamon Gardens*, his second novel, was shortlisted for the Trillium Award. It has been published in the U.S., the U.K., India, and numerous countries in Europe.

Shyam Selvadurai lives in Toronto, where he is at work on a new novel.